HOSTS OF GHOSTS

Cover: Small carving located in a secret place on one of the buildings featured in this book. We call him Hog.

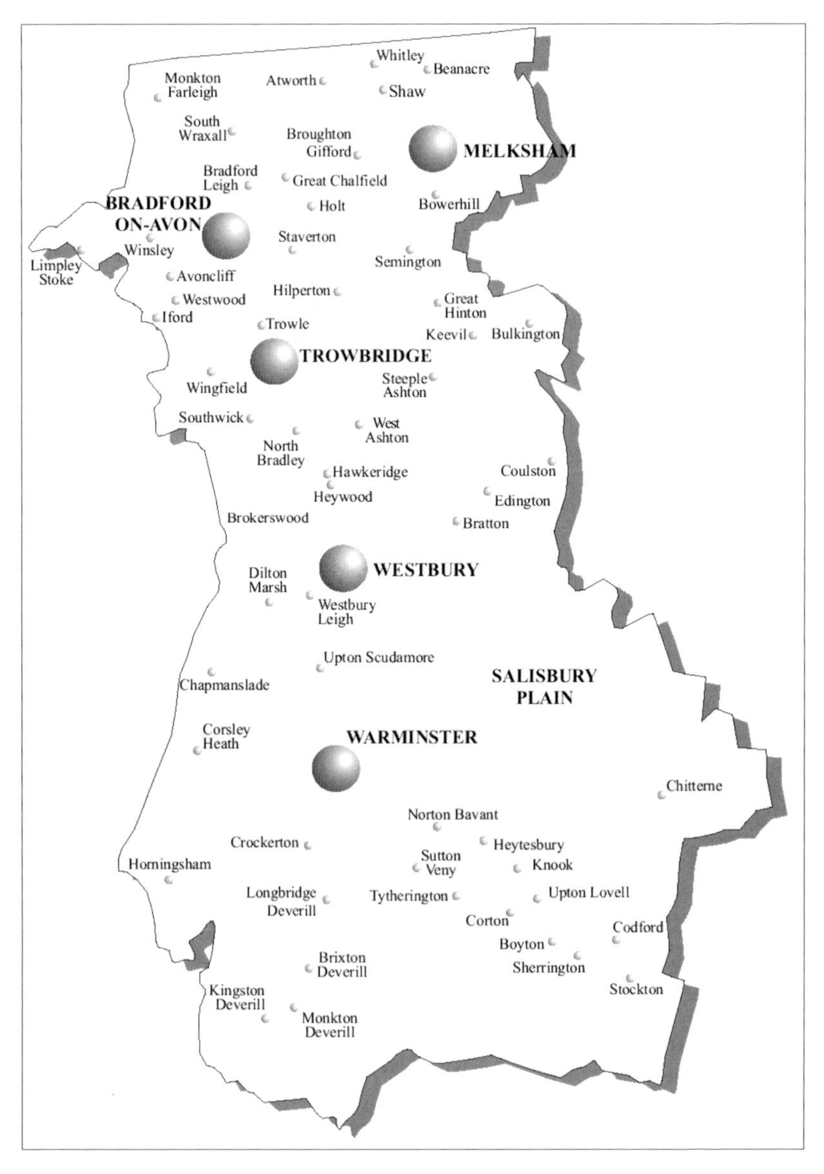

MAP OF WEST WILTSHIRE

HOSTS of GHOSTS

Margaret Dobson
&
Simone Brightstein

EX LIBRIS PRESS

Published in 2005 by
EX LIBRIS PRESS
16A St John's Road
St Helier
Jersey JE2 3LD

Origination by Ex Libris Press

Printed in Britain by
Cromwell Press
Trowbridge, Wiltshire

Typeset in Plantin and Skia;
headings in Papyrus

ISBN 1 990341 29 9

CONTENTS

The Bones of the Book

It was agreed at the outset that material for the book would be drawn only from residents of West Wiltshire, which includes the five towns of Bradford on Avon, Melksham, Trowbridge, Warminster and Westbury and the villages and hamlets within that area.

Many stories had already accrued, but more were needed. The local media were most co-operative in providing articles and radio broadcasts, asking for people with first-person experiences of the paranormal to come forward. The response from these was excellent but the word of mouth reaction was even greater.

The authors divided the workload as follows: contributors were visited by Maggie or Simone and their experiences were tape-recorded. From these conversations, transcripts were made and given to the contributors for their approval. Simone turned the transcripts into first-person stories which were again submitted to the donors before being finalised.

Maggie researched and wrote the commentary, which included the introduction, the historical and scientific data which opens and closes each section and the conclusion. She also selected and interviewed the specialists whose theories highlight many aspects of the narratives. The resultant material was incorporated into the commentary.

Both writers worked together on the merging and proofing of the material and collaborated with Ritka Carr and Jackie Tollit on cover design and photography.

Margaret Dobson
Simone Brightstein
Bradford on Avon
September 2005

Introduction

West Wiltshire is an ancient place. People were wandering over its hills and along its river valleys countless centuries ago. All five of our towns – Bradford on Avon, Melksham, Trowbridge, Warminster and Westbury – became settlements in Saxon times and many of our villages and hamlets can claim their own long histories.

Residents of West Wiltshire delight in its countryside, its old buildings and the sense of history which seems to be part of every town and village. Wide, straight modern routes are very convenient, but somehow quirky, winding roads can be more interesting. For many of us it is this sense of the past and the knowledge that so many generations have lived in these same places, that provides an extra interest and dimension to our enjoyment of the area.

The ways in which earlier generations have created these roads, lanes and buildings is clear for all to see. The question is whether they have also left other more intangible records of their existences, emanations from the past which sometimes make themselves apparent to people who live here now. Consider the millions of DNA particles, each one carrying the imprint of the human body it came from, which must have accumulated through the centuries in every nook and cranny. Matter is indestructible. Those infinitesimal resonances of past generations may still be around – somewhere.

The stories which make up the body of this book suggest that previous generations do still impinge on the present from time to time, although how – or even whether – this could really be the case is a matter for hot debate.

This book does not claim that ghosts exist. You are not being presented with folklore or hearsay, nor is anything invented – far from it. All the stories which follow are first hand accounts from people living in West Wiltshire. Their experiences are varied: some are simple, others more complex. But they all contribute to the same hypothesis: that there is an unknown world which sometimes impinges upon the amazing planet we inhabit.

Vision & Sound

Sally – Andrew – Shaun Ogbourne – Mary M.
Vivien – Hemma – Gill – Jenny – Vernon – Jeannie
Michelle – Sue S. – Jean – William – Piers Bizony

Many contributors to this book have declared a disbelief in ghosts before their strange encounters occurred. Often the event was a long time ago, yet there is a very clear recall of what happened; an episode which remains in sharp detail. For many it was a private experience, kept secret until now. But, unlike some of the narrators of these stories, here is someone who welcomes ghosts and has had a considerable number of experiences with the paranormal.

SALLY

I have had a number of ghostly experiences over the years and I have a theory that many phantom sightings are like recordings of traumatic events, locked into stones such as quartz or other transmitting materials, and released as and when conditions allow. I have two stories to relate here and this first one certainly fits my hypothesis.

A friend of mine owned a haunted chair and although he never saw anything, it always made him feel uncomfortable. Knowing of my interest in antiques, he asked me to caretake it for him and I agreed to do so.

It was a handsome piece of furniture, a carved oak wainscot chair, dated from about 1670. After it was in my house for a short time, I became aware that there was an atmosphere about this chair – it definitely felt odd. I thought it might have been power of suggestion because Roger, my friend, had been so unhappy with it, but within two months' time, I had a sighting.

The chair was positioned so that its back was to whoever entered the room. One day, as I came through the door, I found somebody sitting in the chair and as I moved into the room, I saw that it was a man, dressed in a long, scruffy looking nightshirt, with a nightcap on his matted silver hair. His left leg was stuck out in front of him, resting on something that I couldn't see. It was massively swollen with tight, bright red shiny skin – very angry looking – and there was a filthy rag tied around the foot. The thought came to mind that he might be suffering with gout. He had a pipe loosely held in his left hand, which rested on the arm of the chair.

"Oh, my God!" I thought, as I went further in; as I did so, he turned towards me and I saw his eyes which were blue, but rheumy and red-rimmed. I felt that he might be aware of my presence but, at that moment, I heard a sound like the popping of a cork and he was gone. I sat down in the now empty chair and tried to pick up a feeling of him, but there was nothing.

The man in the chair was seen on seven or eight different occasions: mostly by me, but twice by my husband and once by my daughter, Pam. We called him 'Will' – the name had just come into my head – and we always referred to the chair as 'Will's chair.' Several other people have been aware that somebody was in the chair and quite often, somebody would go to sit in it and suddenly stand up and say, "Oh, I thought I was sitting on a cat or something." Some would sit down again, but many found it too uncomfortable.

Roger sold the chair a few years ago and I was very sorry to see it go. The present owners have no belief in otherworldly things and to my knowledge have had no manifestations of any kind.

Sally's interest in ghostly experiences is well established at the beginning of her account and perhaps that is why she was so ready to take care of a haunted chair. Most of us would be rather wary of sitting in that chair after seeing such an unprepossessing occupant, but Sally tries to get him back. Any suggestions that this is her imagination at work does not fit in with the sightings by other members of her family. Most intriguing of all are the responses of visitors: how could the seat of a seventeenth century chair make people think they were sitting on a cat?

This piece of furniture must have been a great point of interest and discussion throughout its time in Sally's possession. But it is not uncommon for people to keep their experiences to themselves, only revealing them later when the time seems right. Andrew's story is an example.

ANDREW

I work as a decorator and, about five years ago, I was painting a cottage that belongs to parents of a friend of mine. The cottage is about two or three hundred years old and it was a farmworker's house. The owner's son and I put a new extension on the side and, although I know that things sometimes occur when you change an existing building, nothing happened at that time. It was later, when I was in the house on my own, that I had a strange sighting.

I was decorating in the hallway of the new extension and I heard a door shut. None of the other doors or windows in the house were open and the owners were away. I went to check on this bathroom door, which was normally left open and, sure enough, it was closed. It made me a bit on edge, but I went back to work and, while I was at the bottom of the stairs in the hall, I felt like somebody was stood behind me, watching me. I turned around and saw what appeared to be an old lady dressed in grey and black. I only saw her for a moment or two, but it was enough to give me the shivers.

I didn't say anything about it to anybody, but a few weeks later I was having dinner with the owners. Something came up and they said, "Oh, all sorts of strange things happen in this house." and I said, "What do you mean?"

"Oh," she said, "plates drop off shelves and things like that."

"Well," I said, "the other day when I was here, the door shut in the bathroom, you know, and there wasn't anybody else here, no wind or anything. And she said, "It's quite common for doors to shut by themselves here."

"I haven't said anything until now and it might sound stupid, but I thought I saw someone the other day."

"What did the person look like?"

"It was an old lady, dressed in black clothes – grey and black is all I can remember."

"Oh, we've seen her as well, we've seen her quite often, you know."

And that was it, really, this old lady, stood behind me in the corner, watching me paint, maybe trying to see whether the job was a good one or not. She was probably looking at the tin of Dulux paint and thinking, "They didn't use to use that in my day."

The family wasn't at all troubled by what I'd told them and when I delved further into things I talked to their daughter, Teresa, the friend I mentioned earlier. She told me that when they lived in the main farmhouse all sorts of things went bump in the night, but it was something the family had grown up with so they weren't particularly perturbed – it was just strange things that happened now and again.

Shaun Ogbourne, a dowsing investigator with many years experience, observes that many of the events in this book took place when the narrator was in a relaxed frame of mind. Andrew was doing a job he was very used to, so his mind was probably open to other influences.

Like Andrew, Mary M, who was on a social visit, was also in a receptive state.

MARY M.

In 1985 I came from Ireland to live in Bradford on Avon to be near my daughter and son-in law. They lived in a listed cottage on Market Street and I took a place not far from there.

One afternoon, they had several people visiting, including me. They were all talking and I was just sitting back and listening, not really taking part. There's a staircase with a banister, running up into the sitting room, and suddenly I was aware of a man opposite me on the stairwell, which means, really, that he was poised on thin air. The banister seemed to have disappeared so I had a very clear view of him.

He had a long face and a long nose, too. His eyes were round and blue and his large mouth had a set of very big teeth. His hair was coarse and light brown, partly bleached blond by the sun, cut with a fringe and of a length that was just below his ears. He wore a white, full-sleeved shirt of rather fine material, tucked into dark brown trousers and he stood, leaning over a workbench with his arms slightly outstretched, as if he was working at something.

I wasn't surprised or alarmed and the others were carrying on with their conversation, completely oblivious, even though they were sitting practically right up against him. I sat and watched him for about five minutes and then he disappeared.

I didn't say anything to anybody at that point, I suppose I

thought it would be foolish of me to break into their conversation. When I got home, I immediately wrote the experience down and drew a simple sketch of the man, while everything was still fresh.

I did tell Sylvia what had happened but neither she nor Dennis ever saw anything in all the time they lived there. I discovered that there was no staircase originally, so where he stood had once been part of the room.

My notes and the sketch were misplaced for some time and I only found them again recently, but the event had always stayed vividly in my mind.

Mary M saw this as a very private experience and did not attempt to bring others in the room into the event. Andrew was only aware of the colours his apparition was wearing, but Mary was amazingly explicit. This was surely no impromptu arrangement of shadows which might be surmised to be a figure. She saw a man with such clarity that she could observe the coarseness of his hair, the design of his shirt and the fineness of the material from which it was made. He was busy about his work and was suspended in the stairwell – which seems impossible.

But the cottage has been extensively altered in the last hundred years. Originally there was no staircase to this upstairs room and there would have been a solid floor where the man, unaware of Mary, was working away in his own world.

There are more instances of sightings where the figure appears to be inhabiting a different level in a different world. The next story comes from another old area in the same town but this time there are observations from three different people.

VIVIEN

It was either late winter in ninety-one or early in ninety-two when I received the deeds to my recently purchased house. It is part of a row of former weavers' cottages that front onto a steep little hill and back onto a path that leads to their gardens – a beautifully secret spot that characterises the charm of Bradford on Avon.

I was completely alone on that day; my neighbours on one side were on holiday and those on the other side were weekenders – nobody in the row but me. I sat at my table, looking at the deeds and thinking about the history of the house when I became aware that something was passing the kitchen window. I looked up, saw a figure go by and thought: "We have an intruder!"

I rushed out of the back door but there was nobody there. The gate to the back was locked, so nobody could have got in – or out. Then I suddenly realised that I hadn't seen a real person.

If someone walks by our back window you see the whole body, but only from the neck down because the path is too high to see anyone's head; I had seen only the upper part of this man. He was a light grey colour and was wearing a kind of peaked cap. I could see the shoulders and just down to the waist. I felt quite spooked about this and I thought "I've seen a ghost – but I don't know if I believe in them." Then I realised that he hadn't been walking in the normal way, but had glided past the window. I got the feeling that he had been walking along the back of our buildings from somewhere further along the street.

Although I felt a bit weird about this sighting, it had a good feeling about it, as if it was a happy occasion. I haven't seen that particular figure again, although there have been other events involving myself, friends and neighbours.

HEMMA

I never thought much about this incident until my neighbour, Viv, said that she thought she'd seen some people going by on the back lane. Then I remembered that about two years ago, I was in my kitchen, doing whatever you do, and I thought I saw one – possibly two – people walking past my window from the gate to the house of my neighbour on the other side.

It was late afternoon in the winter and I thought it was a funny time for people to be wandering around out there, so I stayed at the window, but they never returned along the path. I remember thinking that they must have been ghosts. They were small people and, on looking back, I realise that I've seen this kind of thing before and thought, "Who's gone by there?" and then said to myself, "Oh, it's just my neighbour emptying the compost," but late on a winter's day is a strange time to do the compost – and sometimes these sightings happened when my neighbours weren't there.

GILL

Viv and I live together, next door to Hemma. The kitchens of all the houses in our row look out on the back path and gardens and there's a gate at the back which is always kept locked, so we never have strangers passing by.

One day, about two years ago, I was alone in the kitchen and nobody was in the back area of the houses. I was busy preparing a meal and I was just aware of someone passing by the window. I thought it was strange because I was so sure nobody else was around, but there was a man in a white shirt, and with grey hair, neatly tied back. He was going from our right-hand neighbour's house towards the gate.

I quickly went to the back door and looked out but couldn't see anyone, even though nobody could have reached the gate in that time.

I had a sort of warm feeling and I thought, "I wonder if that was Viv's ghost?"

Last summer, Viv and I bought the neighbour's house and since then, several times when I've been in the kitchen, I've seen what I can only describe as the flash of a white figure in the garden. Whoever it is, he seems to be very much at home here.

The setting of the next story is also that of an ancient cottage, this time in the village of Holt but with similarities to the happenings on the garden path in Bradford on Avon.

JENNY

For several years – four or five, I'd say – I lived in an ancient cottage in the village of Holt.

It was filled with spirits: my children were particularly aware of them and very sympathetic about them. I believe they even saw the ghost of a Roman soldier at one time.

Spirits always move as if the place they inhabit still had the same geographical layout and the same ground level as in their time. In the Victorian era, a room was added to the original building, taking away some of the garden space. One of our ghosts, a gardener who died before the addition had been put on, was still to be seen, walking through the Victorian sitting room. pushing an old-fashioned wheelbarrow. His feet were invisible, hidden below the floorboards at the garden level he would have walked on. He never troubled us, just trundled through the room, completely unaware that his garden was long gone.

Vernon's experience, which forms the next story, has never been explained in rational terms and still provokes thoughtful speculation.

VERNON

This isn't a story about a ghost as such but it concerns a strange sight that I've never been able to explain.

I live in Church Street, Bradford on Avon. The house is late seventeenth century with what we believe is a sixteenth century fireplace and I've been told that there was probably an earlier house on the site. My land, which I think was glebe land, contains many interesting things. I've dug up marbles and have quite a collection of them, both glass and clay; an old military button from the Thirteenth Light Dragoons and, over a long period of time, I have unearthed many human bones. Initially I reported the discovery of these bones to the police who promptly took them away but subsequently returned them as they said they were over a hundred years old and therefore they weren't interested in them and I buried them in the churchyard.

In the summer of 1970, I was sitting in the living room with a friend who was visiting; she was diagonally across from me and we could both see the door, which was to my left. I was just staring into space when I suddenly noticed what looked rather like a sparkler that a child would hold on Bonfire Night. It was dancing up and down the hinge side of the door and although it only lasted for three or four seconds, it was very vivid. I don't believe it was anything to do with electricity, because wood isn't a conductor and, although there's a light socket near the door now, it wasn't there in those days.

I turned to my friend and said, "Did you see what I've just seen?'

"Yes," she replied.

We both sat speechless for a moment or two. Neither of us felt frightened in any way and I sensed that, whatever it was, was benign, but it was a pretty peculiar experience. It's never happened again, but I've often thought of it and wondered what it was.

An occurrence such as the one experienced by Vernon and his friend might come within the area of 'orbs' – i.e. mobile luminous circles of light. These oft-recorded phenomena are well known to followers of the paranormal and are currently under detailed investigation by 'OrbStudy'. Analyses of their experiments continue and have produced many scientific hypotheses. Their reports are published on the Internet.

Most of the accounts in this Vision and Sound section deal with one or the other of these senses. Jeannie's story differs in that both sound and sight are very much present.

JEANNIE

My parents and I lived up above one of the shops in Silver Street, twenty-five years ago. It was an old building and the flat had wooden floorboards and heavy doors with wooden latches.

On this particular night, I was getting ready for bed and I heard footsteps outside my bedroom door. Thinking it was one of my parents, I called out "Good night", but got no response. Shortly after I heard the latch on my door lift, but nobody came in and the door stayed shut.

The room had two windows, both of which were closed. A few minutes later, the door latch lifted again, the curtains, which were very heavy, blew inwards as if in a wind and the room turned cold for a moment, as if you'd opened and closed a freezer door.

Uneasy, I turned around in my chair and saw an old woman sitting in a corner of the room. She looked perfectly solid and was wearing a long, dark dress. She was quite a chunky little woman and, although her head was down so I couldn't see her features, I thought that my grandmother, whom I'd never met, might have looked like that.

I knew I was wide awake and not dreaming this, but I scolded myself, saying "You've got too vivid an imagination, my girl." and I never told anyone what had happened.

Two years later, my parents had moved down to Devon, but I stayed in the flat. I had a friend from Spain visiting me and she stayed in that room but I didn't tell her what had happened to me in there. On her second night, she was sitting at the dressing table; although all the floors had been carpeted by then, she heard someone in the hall walking as if on wooden floorboards and then she experienced exactly the same events that had happened to me.

As I said, I hadn't been frightened by what happened because I'd told myself it was my over-active imagination, but now I knew that it was nothing of the kind. My friend, who had had other ghostly experiences, was quite excited about the encounter.

I no longer live in Bradford on Avon and don't know if any later residents of that flat have had similar happenings.

Although it happened long ago, Jeannie's memory of her visitation remains vivid, as is the case with all the contributors to this book. Michelle's frightening experience, which took place at the Westbury Tourist Information Centre, clearly illustrates this.

MICHELLE

I used to be the manager of the Westbury Tourist Information Centre. It shares the building known as Westbury House with the Library and. in addition to my other duties, I had the responsibility for security.

The T.I.C. closed at 4:30 in the afternoon but I was organising an upcoming event, so I was working late and, I thought, was alone in the building as the Library would have been closed for the night too.

It was about 7.30 p.m. and I was deep in paper work when all of a sudden there was a lot of noise coming from the top floor: opening and closing of doors, footsteps, walking and running, piano music, violin playing, singing and dancing – it was an awful racket.

I was quite cross, because my first thought was that the librarians were having a managers' meeting and hadn't bothered to tell me. I went over to the Library side and, to my surprise, found all the lights off. Then it occurred to me that children might have got in at the back door, so I turned one light on in the Library and headed off to check the back area. As I went, I called the names of the librarians and the caretaker as well, but the festivities upstairs carried on and I had no response. The music was like something you'd have heard on the TV show of *Pride And Prejudice.* It was a lively polka and you could hear the sounds of dancing feet. It was very jolly, but so loud – *dreadfully* loud.

When I reached the stairs, the noise stopped as if a switch had been thrown and then somebody came running down the stairs. I say somebody, because, although I couldn't see anything, they were definitely footsteps – feminine footsteps and they sounded as if the person was wearing a pair of dancing slippers. They stopped on a stair near the bottom and then they *jumped* from the step to the ground right in front of me.

I stood there, frozen to the floor for what seemed like an age, terrified that somebody was going to appear in front of me, but nobody did. Finally I was able to move and move I did, back to the T.I.C., turning on lights as I went, back through the Library and into the T.I.C. where I worked really fast – took my bag, grabbed as much material as I could in my hands and took it to the main entrance. I put everything outside the door, which I had to keep propping open, then – back to the Library where I turned off the lights, did a security check and left as quickly as possible.

When I got home, I told Martyn, my husband, what had happened. I was in quite a state because it had been so frightening and so totally unexpected. He just said, "hmm...hmm." The next day I mentioned it to the librarians and they said that they'd all had similar experiences. They were very cavalier about it.

A few weeks later, again it was a Wednesday, there was a visiting caretaker because our regular had gone on holiday. This woman arrived at the same time as I, about 8:30 a.m.; we said "Good morning", I unlocked the door and we went in, me to my office and she to the second floor to begin cleaning.

About ten minutes later, she came to me and said, "Is there someone else in the building?"

"No," I replied and she whispered, "Somebody's walking up on the third floor, walking up and down and opening the doors. I did call up there, but nobody answered me."

"Oh," I said," that's the ghost, don't worry about it." I was quite flippant about it, just as the librarians had been.

"Nobody told me that there's a ghost here," she said.

"Oh, everyone knows there's a ghost. I shouldn't worry about it – she won't harm you."

But she refused to do any more cleaning and left.

Nothing else happened during the rest of the time that I worked at the Tourist Information Centre. Sometimes I'd get a sort of goosepimply feeling, but the big party never happened again.

A sceptic might find explanation from external noises – a passing car with its radio blaring, for example – but that would not fit in with the length of time the sounds continued. Note also Michelle's specific description of the kind of music and the ways in which the footsteps moved. These vivid details are an auditory match for the visual details in other stories. These events also seem to be ones which recur, as Michelle's colleagues confirmed. Moreover the visiting caretaker was so affected that she refused to work there again.

Unlike Michelle, Sue S's experience in the next story was shared by her husband who was far from frozen. He was determined to locate the source of the unexpected and unwelcome footsteps in their house and sort it all out.

SUE S.

We bought the house in Broughton Gifford in 1967. It was an old wheelwright's cottage – an absolute wreck, but my husband was a builder and he knew what he was looking for. We paid twelve hundred pounds for it and it was so bad that Halifax wouldn't give us a mortgage. Luckily we went to Abbey National and they could see the potential in it.

My husband, Colin, worked on the house in the evenings for two years before we actually moved in. There was no gas or electric, so he used a Tilley lamp and he'd say, "You know, it ain't half spooky working there at Tilley light."

He dug new foundations, installed new electrics, made a kitchen where there was just a lean-to and put a new bathroom above the kitchen. The lounge was running in water, so he had to dig it all out and damp proof it and after that he put new plaster on all the walls in the lounge, the halls and the dining room and hung new doors everywhere. By the time he was finished, we had a lovely house and no mistake.

The first year we were living there, we visited some friends one evening who lived just across the road. When we left and got back to our front door, Colin said, "There's somebody in the house – listen!" We could hear heavy footsteps walking across our landing. We had one of those old-fashioned turn keys and Colin put it in the lock and turned it very quietly. He crept into the dining room, picked up the poker and chased up the stairs ten at a time, all ready to give whoever what for – but there was nobody there.

I was still stood outside, petrified with worry that whoever was in the house would turn on Colin but he came back downstairs all of a piece. "Well," he said, " that's funny! You heard it, didn't you?"

"Yes," I said, " 'course I heard it."

"I expect it was the neighbour getting out of bed and perhaps walking along her landing," said Colin and I said, "Well, I wouldn't have thought so, because our walls are eighteen inches thick and there's a four-inch gap between her house and ours."

What it was, we never knew.

Contributors' stories frequently contain reference to sound in conjunction with other strange happenings:

JEAN

We called it Willow Cottage and even though it was just a semi-detached house on the Trowbridge Road it had large grounds and a well. We moved there in 1973 and strange things began happening right away: lights going on and off for no reason; icy cold spots in parts of the house and often a strong feeling that somebody was behind you. Strangely enough, it wasn't unpleasant and not even the children were frightened.

I think it must have been an inn at one time, when both houses were one building, because at night we used to hear an awful lot of heavy footsteps going up and down the stairs. There was drumming, too, at the back of the house and when new people moved to the other side, I said to my husband, "When I get to know them, I'm gong to ask if they hear this drummer boy." When I met my neighbour, I said, "I hope you don't think I'm a bit doolally, but have you ever heard any drumming and marching at night?" And she said, "Yes, I have." So I felt much better because I'd had so much a feeling of *"Is it me?"*

However much rational explanation a sceptic might look for here, he would have difficulty in brushing away the next story when two boys ventured into Keevil airfield one night.

WILLIAM

It all started – well, it didn't actually *start*, it just *happened*. It was fifty years ago, when I lived in the village of Steeple Ashton. My house was close to Keevil airfield; it was all empty then, long deserted. A deserted airfield is an eerie place at night; you get foxes howling and owls hooting, but my friends and I used to go out there on our bikes, mooching around the various huts as young lads do.

We were all model aircraft builders but this was in the early fifties when materials were still in short supply. In one of those huts were two long chart tables, set at an angle in the wall and they were ideal building boards. "Right," we said, "we'll have them."

My friend, Tom, and I went down on the airfield one evening, must have been late September, early October; it was getting dark, but you could still see where to pedal your bike. We had a torch and we went into the hut and began unscrewing all the brackets, working by torchlight. It took a while but we finally got those two beautiful tops off and up we stood, ready to go.

Then, oh, God! We heard a car draw up outside. It had to be the police. Caught red-handed! Caught *red-handed!* There was a slamming of car doors and then men, at least three of them, came towards the hut. We could hear their boots crunching on the gravelly bit of path, coming through the doorway and then clumping along the main passageway. We heard them talking, even though we couldn't make out what they were saying. There was a corridor leading off the main passage; we were on that one, in the second room down and the pitch of their voices changed as they came towards us. We just looked at each other, struck dumb with fright – caught red-handed – what would the villagers say? In a small place like that, gossip stays around for years and we'd always be branded as the lads that stole from the airfield.

We stared at the door, expecting to see three policemen come through it; they were only a yard away...a step away...we could hear them as plain as day, their boots on the concrete floor. And then, they just faded away; there wasn't an abrupt cut off, they simply *fa-a-ded* away. The voices – the footsteps – *gone.*

Tom and I gawped at each other. "Did you hear what I heard?"

"Yes."

We waited, stock still, for a couple of minutes, then peeped round the door: nobody there. *Absolutely* nothing there!

Hearts a-pounding, we sidled out into the passageway and crept along to our bicycles which were just inside the doorway. There wasn't a sound, nor was there a soul about and when we got to the front door there was no car – nothing.

We were off – left the boards behind, scrambled onto our bikes and we were gone. Now, we weren't children, we were young men around seventeen or eighteen, but we felt quite shaken and when we got back to my house, we sat down, had a cup of tea and talked it over.

Both Tom and I agreed that our first thought had been that it was the police who, having spotted somebody hanging around the airfield, had charged out in their car and barrelled into the hut to grab us. But we realised fairly quickly that no car lights had passed the window, we'd seen no shadow and, instead of screeching to a halt as you'd expect a police car on the chase to do, it had *rolled* to a halt with a bit of a crunch of gravel under the tyres. We agreed that we'd heard at least three doors slamming and that at least three men had got out of the car. We could hear the boots and you know when three or four men are talking as opposed to two – there's that gobbledegook of chatter without being able to hear what was being said.

As we talked about it and calmed down a bit, we also realised that it wasn't police *charging* down the corridor, but men *walking* down it; you could picture them chatting to each other over their shoulders. And the only conclusion we could come to was that they were a crew of airmen. We know the car had no lights and in wartime, they all drove with dimmers on. If it had been the police, we would have seen lights for certain. You'd never drive around those narrow roads without headlights on; you'd go off the edge too easily. And the police would never have faded into thin air.

Tom and I talked about it a few times afterwards, but it was one of those things we didn't bring up very often. Oh, once or twice, especially if we had a group of friends down on the airfield flying model planes, we'd say, "Remember this?"

"Oh, yes, yes."

But I didn't tell many people at the time because I thought it was a daft thing to say. Who's going to believe you? And, of course, in the village, if you say something silly, it's never forgotten, you see, and you'd always be looked upon as that daft bloke who heard the ghosts in the airfield.

Sometimes, when I tell this story, someone will say it was a great experience and on reflection, it is, but at the time, my God were we *frightened*! We didn't go near that airfield again for at least a year.

I tell you this as absolute gospel. I'll swear on a stack of bibles that it is true and I can assure you – they were there; those men were in that corridor. I would put my *life* on it.

I was asked if I'd ever heard of anyone else having a similar experience. I haven't, but I'd like to know if anyone has. As I said, the airfield is a frightening place at night: I lived very near the airfield boundary, so I know what a lonely spot it is and I wouldn't live down there again if you gave the house to me.

The impact on William and Tom was profound and has stayed with them all their lives. A compelling power seems to have been at work. The amount of human energy expended over countless generations is surely enormous and may still be present. Keevil airfield must have been a centre for all kinds of intense activity during the Second World War. Is it possible, for example that a great charge of human emotion could be retained in old areas, whether buildings or land?

Such an imprint could have created the boys' experience. This might sound fanciful but physical forces do leave their mark. When rocks are liquefied, the atoms within them are still loose; the iron atoms become aligned along lines of magnetic force and then, as the rock hardens, they are literally frozen into place. Scientific analysis of rocks shows where magnetic North was at the time when, as magma, the rocks emerged onto the surface of our planet. The imprint is there forever.

In much the same way paranormal imprints may surface under appropriate conditions. Manifestations come in many forms and we may never know how they occur. There is so much we do not know. Can we really be surrounded by other worlds of which we know nothing? Common sense says that this is impossible. But common sense can be very misleading. Our bodies tell us that we live in a stable world where the ground stays steady under our feet. Cushioned by the earth's atmosphere we feel that the earth is static in space. We are programmed to take this for granted – any other sensations would be unbearable. Yet in fact the earth is rotating on its axis every 24 hours and we are whirling around the sun at 67,000 miles per hour. What we experience as reassuringly stable is not so at all.

Modern technology enables scientists to look into the minuscule particles from which the universe is made. A 'quantum' is the smallest unit of something it is possible to have – hence the term 'Quantum Physics'. No one, not even the physicists themselves, can completely understand this uncharted scientific world, but quantum physics has taken knowledge of the universe into new and terrifying levels of investigation.

Eminent scientist Werner Heisenberg, who was a pioneer in the study of quantum physics as it developed in the twentieth century, says: "If anyone thinks they understand quantum physics, they must be *mad* because quantum physics defies all of our normal expectations about the world" Nowadays quantum physics seems to be part of almost every scientific investigation into the mechanics of the universe.

Piers Bizony helps to clarify this abstruse subject for the layman:

> Until the end of the nineteenth century, everybody thought the world was made out of solid things that you could definitely touch and play with and cut up with a knife. The world was solid and moved forward in time and there was one universe. So, when in the early part of the twentieth century it was found that sub-components of atoms – electrons and such – could be in two places at once and could go backwards

> in time, it worried the classical scientists. Einstein himself was appalled. He didn't like the idea that any part of nature could be in two places at once.
>
> Still, this was established theoretically at the time and has recently been confirmed by experiment. Big things behave in ways we understand. Planets go round the sun in a certain direction; we know exactly where Jupiter will be on April the third at eight-thirty in the evening. But with individual atoms or their components, those rules are thrown out of the window. Things that are supposed to go forward, go backward; things that should be here are there, and things that should be one thing, turn into multiple entities. So we have quantum physics – the study of how very, very, very small things behave.
>
> When you've got a beaker of mercury you can say: "I've got exactly one litre of mercury here." But if you try to cut the mercury up with a tiny little razor blade, to get the smallest piece of it, the little beads will fly all over the place. When you look at anything at the atomic level or smaller and try to isolate a single little chunk, these tiny, tiny bits that make up a world will squiggle around like droplets of mercury if you try to pin them down.

This is all very heady stuff and difficult for non-scientists to follow. But what it does, incontrovertibly, is to unsettle any confidence we may have that the world we live in is predictable, a place where all can be explained by the laws of physics. The Newtonian and Cartesian laws are no longer sufficient to explain the universe and we cannot separate ourselves and our world from the chaotic and unpredictable universe in which we have our being.

Staircase at Westbury House, Westbury from the ghost's perspective *(See Michelle's story, page 23)*

Overhead view of the Trowbridge Castle excavations, showing many of the graves with some skeletons still in situ. The arrow in the upper left hand corner indicates the back of Peewee's Real Ale Bar.
(See Peewee's story, page 35)

Some of the skeletons from one of the excavations on the site of Trowbridge Castle, where The Shires Shopping Centre now stands.

The above two photographs published through the courtesy of Wessex Archeology

Left: Reconstruction of the contents of Peewee's cellar before the upheaval, with all items in their usual places

Below: The disorder that Peewee found. Note the coins still suspended in the upside down tin

Kevin's alcove, in the Tithe Barn, Bradford on Avon: a large oval recess in the south wall, possibly created as part of a primitive method of weighing sacks of grain or other materials (See Kevin's story, page 61)

Ali's mirror, a treasure from her grandmother (See Ali's story, page 75)

POLTERGEISTS

Peewee – Zoe – Buzz – Shaun D – Frances – Shaun L
Jenny G – Rob – Judith – Elizabeth
Florence – Enid – Roger – Eleanor Macbeth
Piers Bizony – Shaun Ogbourne

Manifestations do not only occur in a visual or auditory manner. They can appear in other aspects which seem to be devised by some mischievous invisible presence. The result is that the person might decide that a preternatural being is present. Responses to such weird events vary: some people remain disconcerted while others accept the happenings as part of the building's character.

It is frequently remarked that someone buying a house will have an immediate feeling about the property they have just entered. Perhaps it is simply created by identifiable features in the house itself. Yet what one person dismisses as unacceptable in a new home another might see as an ideal purchase. It seems that we are likely to respond to intangibles in a place as much as to its physical appearance. It is something personal, intuitive and individual. Is it some form of psychic awareness which we all have to some extent?

PEEWEE

Peewee's Real Ale Bar was a public house I ran in Trowbridge for nineteen years. It's a reasonably old building – early eighteenth century – but it sits on the site of Trowbridge Castle. In the late 1980s, the Wessex Archaeological Trust carried out a survey of the area which would become the new Shires Shopping Centre. Behind the pub and under the end wall of the building, they found a number of skeletons which were consecrated and reburied in Southwick. But they surmised that some of the skeletons, which are believed to be from around the twelfth century, were right under the foundations at the very back of the pub and couldn't be taken out. They're still *in situ* – still there.

Too many strange things have happened at that pub for me to remember them all, but the ones I'm about to tell you have stayed vivid in my memory and always will.

First there's the case of the missing grill pan: I was living at the pub with Zoe, my partner of that time, back in 1982. We had private accommodation on the first floor – very comfortable. The front room leads off a long, narrow galley kitchen and on this day Zoe was in the front room while I was in the kitchen about to make some toast but, when I went to light the gas, the grill pan wasn't there. Zoe and I searched every inch of the kitchen but we never found the grill pan and I ended up going to Shanley's scrap yard and getting a second-hand pan there.

Later in the year we were putting on a pantomime for charity and we had the rear bar set up theatre style. On the opening day, a hot water pipe burst and poured down from the loft, through the ceiling and all over the chairs and the stage. It was an absolute disaster and we were lucky that the audience hadn't yet arrived.

I was desperate. A set of plans showed that the hot water tank and its stopcock were enclosed in a floor-to-ceiling partitioned area in the kitchen but the previous owners had covered the partition over with woodchip paper and painted it blue. Zoe and I grabbed kitchen knives and frantically began scraping off the wallpaper. Eventually we got enough off to expose tongue and groove flooring planks, screwed securely together. I managed to heave one of the planks out and, just as the plan showed, there was the water tank with a big red stopcock next to it. I turned the stopcock off and breathed a sigh of relief as the water stopped its downpour. Looking down, I saw, underneath the tank, the grill pan which had gone missing months before. We could never figure out how it got in there.

One regular phenomenon was the cold spot in the back bar. Often, if we had friends staying, the talk would turn to the ghost and when a guest was sceptical, I'd say: "Right – here's a dare for you. We'll stay up here in the lounge; you go down to the pub, into the back bar. You'll find a set of optics there: to use them, your back will be to the pub. I'll have a large whiskey, Zoe will want vodka and coke, have what you'd like for yourself – but you *must* pour them without turning to look behind you.

Off he'd go, full of confidence, but in minutes he'd scuttle back saying: "I can't do it – I can't do it – it's so *cold* down there!" What he felt was an indescribably icy chill that gave the shudders to everyone who experienced it.

In the rear bar is a stone pillar with a framed copy of the Magna Carta on it. One night, after hours, there was a group of us in the room; Zoe, my friend Buzz, the news editor of the *Wiltshire Times*, and his wife. We were nattering away when suddenly there was a huge smashing noise. We all spun round on our bar stools: the Magna Carta had flown the entire width of that big room, hit the wall on the other side and now lay on the ground. We sat staring at it and at each other, more than a little bit shaken.

Lots of smaller things happened, peppered throughout the years between the really major events. One Saturday afternoon, an ashtray levitated in full view of the customers sat around the table – it rose, threw itself through the air and then emptied itself on the floor. Everybody saw it happen; they believed that someone threw it – but no, it *did* levitate. Just a few days later, a jukebox speaker that was suspended on the wall came off its mounting. The wooden encased speaker was about three pounds in weight and should have fallen straight down to the floor, but instead it defied gravity and sailed in an arc through the air to land about twelve feet away – miraculously undamaged.

In later years, after closing time, I would sit with my friend Nigel the doorman and wait for his taxi. We'd be in the rear bar having a wind-down drink and, on that right hand corner, the ashtrays on the table would skitter about. They were thirty feet away and we'd hear *tck-tck-tck* as they danced around. We got so used to it, we'd ask whoever it was to come and join us.

In the summer of '82 we made television news when a routine delivery from Whitbreads Brewery caused a rather dramatic disturbance.

We'd had an outside event and, as was usual, bought a number of 24-can cases with the understanding that any unused cases would be returned. We had about fifteen cases to go back and, on the next Whitbreads run, the draymen were to take the cases away.

You walk straight into the cellar which is at ground level and is about twelve foot square. The cases for return were stacked against the far wall, so the two draymen and I formed a chain; one of them stood at the stack of cases, I was in the middle of the room behind him and the other drayman was outside on the path.

As we were passing the cases out, an empty five-gallon plastic cider barrel rose into the air, hovered briefly and shot between me and the drayman who was lifting the cases out. The container bounced off the wall and jittered all over the floor, about two feet off the ground.

The drayman, who had his back turned, looked around, chuckled and said: "Whas tha do that for, then? That were a bit stupid."

His mate was mouth agape with a face as white as a sheet. "That warn't him, Bert," he said, "That done that by itself – that lifted itself up and it flied between you."

Bert and I joined the drayman outside and saw the cider

container levitate again, ricochet around the walls three times and then fall down.

The draymen went back to the brewery and told their story and I then had a phone call from Whitbread's transport manager who told me that their union would no longer allow the draymen to go into the cellar, only to the door; my staff would have to move everything in or out from there. And that's how the event became a news item on HTV or BBC West – possibly both.

The Psychic Pig Club used to meet across the road from the White Swan. Richard, who was one of my staff members, was going there with me, to catch up with some friends. We'd closed the pub, Richard had come up from the cellar where he'd been washing the last basket of glasses and I went down there to do a security check. I found the place in total chaos and immediately went to Richard: "You've just come out of the cellar," I said, "Why didn't you tell me about this?"

"What?"

"The incredible mess in here."

He went back into the cellar and was absolutely shocked. "It wasn't like this when I came out."

Several cases of shrink wrapped cider in plastic four-and-a-half-pint jugs had been stacked side by side in the corner. On top were three cases of wrapped bottled cider and a stainless steel catering tin, filled with bags of coins that were used to make change. In just two minutes, everything in the cellar had been chaotically rearranged.

The case of cider jugs that would be hardest to move had been pulled out of its stack and was lying on the floor, four feet away. The cases of bottles were on top of each other, upended in the middle of the floor and the catering tin was upside down on a Real Ale barrel with the bags of coins magically suspended inside. The building was locked; nobody but Richard and I were there. The flinging around of those items should have caused considerable noise, but neither of us heard anything.

Many unexplained things happened at that pub: some

frightening, some amusing, some just plain annoying, but they became part of my life and when I moved from there to my present location, when I was about to lock the door, I walked around the building and pleaded with that presence to come with me: "Please, come" I said, " it's not very far away." There I was, like an idiot, telling the air, talking to the corners... "Please – you'd be very welcome. Come with me...please come." But whatever was in that building didn't accept my invitation and I came here alone.

Wherever possible, corroboration is given by the independent evidence from others. In this instance, several people who lived and worked at Peewee's, describe many of the same curious happenings.

Zoe was a partner there for some time and gives us her version of the events.

ZOE

When I was about eighteen, my best friend Alison and I moved into an end terrace house in Trowbridge. It was an ordinary, working class brick house with one unusual feature – a large basement that wasn't accessible from the house itself. You could only get into it by going outside and down some steps to a lower road which ran at right angles to the house. Once there, you could reach the double doors that lead into the basement.

The house was rented by Peewee's Real Ale Bar, a local pub where Ali and I both worked and the basement was used for extra storage as space was very limited at the pub.

Ali and I enjoyed living in the house and have many fond

memories of our time there but the most memorable event was rather sinister. We began to hear noises coming from the basement late at night. The sound was very similar to that of empty metal beer barrels being tossed around by draymen. It was so loud that we thought intruders had got in to the basement, so we would go outside and down the steps to the outside door only to find that it was still padlocked.

The first time it happened we thought that some metal barrels must have been stored there, but when we looked inside the next day, there weren't any. This happened on a regular basis and one time, when some draymen were there to pick up some empty plastic cider barrels, one lifted itself from where it had been placed and flew across the room, narrowly missing one of them. They were extremely freaked out.

Later, I moved into the pub and Peewee and I were convinced that 'Eric', as we had named him, had followed me there. All sorts of mischievous things happened but the strangest was when the grill pan disappeared one day. We searched for it but finally gave up and were totally bemused as to where it could have gone. Many months later the water tank needed some maintenance. It was located in the kitchen, boxed in by panels which were covered in woodchip wallpaper. The only way to get to the tank was to rip open the panels and when we'd removed them we found the grill pan, wedged between the tank and the wall. There was no way anyone could have hidden it there without leaving evidence.

A few years later I moved up North and sometimes I was sure that Eric had followed me there for a while.

Buzz, who knew Peewee's Real Ale Bar over many years, confirms several stories.

BUZZ

It was 1984 and we were sat at Peewee's in the front bar, just to the left of the front door. It was early evening and we were sat in the window. I thought I heard the door handle move, so I turned around to watch for somebody coming in, but nobody did.

I'd watched a couple of times and so had my friend, Alex. I'd asked her if she'd heard the rattle and she said, yes, her attention had been caught by the noise, too. We watched a few minutes more and saw it move. I jumped up, opened the door and looked outside but there was nobody there and no wind that could have caused the noise.

A couple of years later, a group of us had stayed on after hours with Peewee. I was stood facing the bar and I heard a clatter behind me. It was very loud and everyone else heard it, too. We all looked around. There had been a framed copy of the Magna Carta on a pillar at the edge of the room but now it was lying face down in the middle of the floor, which means it had flown over the pool table which is a distance of least eight feet. I picked it up and looked at it and found that the glass wasn't broken. We all immediately identified it as being the poltergeist.

In June of 1989 Peewee was redecorating the front bar. Normally the back bar was closed at lunch time, but they had it open because of the work in the front. I was one of the first people in at lunch time and, although it was a warm day, it was so unbelievably chilly in the back bar that you could see your breath. That cold spot, which many people experienced, was often there.

A long-time staff member, Shaun D experienced the same events and adds his own comments.

SHAUN D.

I was eighteen years old when I began working at Peewee's Real Ale Bar. I lived in the pub too – was there for about eight years – and I carried on working for Peewee after I moved out.

Strange things were always going on: sometimes it was just funny little tricks, like the gas for the barrels being turned off at busy times, especially at Last Orders, or the barrels in the cellar being moved about and all the ashtrays that danced around the tables.

I remember one time when we'd done an outside event and were unloading the leftover cases and barrels. We stacked them just inside the door, Peewee went off with the car and I locked everything up and went back to the bar. It was shut as usual for the afternoon and I went upstairs for a while. When I came back down to open up, everything in the cellar was piled up at the other end of the room in a different order, as though somebody had unloaded it again – neatly done, but not as I'd left it. I asked Peewee if he'd moved the stuff but he'd only just got back from the Cash and Carry. This kind of thing happened a lot, as if whatever did it was saying, "I live here, too, and this is the way *I* want things."

Then there was the cold spot which was between the front and the back bars: it *always* caught me unawares. I'd be down there quite happily on my own, and then oooowwwwahhh – I'd get that shiver down my back and say, "I'm not staying down here too long." It was an unnatural cold, and it felt like somebody was stood behind you. The archaeologists used to come in the pub quite often and they said some of the graveyard went under the back bar and that a big well was just underneath where the pool table stood.

Another incident happened when we had the nightclub. In addition to the regular bar staff, we had a chap who used to come in and help out and he always brought his dog along. The poor thing was old and quite poorly and he used to stay in a dressing room which was at the end of a long corridor.

One night, the fellow went to get his dog and discovered it had died. The next night, we were sitting around after hours as usual. One of the staff hadn't been here the night before and didn't know about the dog's death and he suddenly said, "Who let that dog in here?"

"What dog?" I said.

He pointed to the corridor, "the black dog that just ran across there."

He described my mate's dog and when I told him that it had died the night before he went: "Ooo! Oooohoooo!"

So, like, all these things, they happened and they were just a part of our life here – the barrels moving, the ashtrays, all that. There is one episode, though, that bothers me and that was the grill pan that we found when we were trying to turn off the water. Peewee had told me about it disappearing and then – when it turned up under the hot water tank it was like, "Oh, my God – look at *that*!" It was fifteen years ago and it still gives me goose pimples every time I think about it.

The natural response to anyone's description of strange happenings is usually – "What physical evidence do you have to support your claims?" Peewee's account includes references to a number of solid objects which behaved in unusual ways. Among others there is the grill pan which was discovered months later in a previously unknown place, the jiggling ashtrays, the bar optics which turned off at awkward moments and the inexplicable chaos in the cellar. Shaun's contribution is important because it was given quite independently of Peewee's story. Zoe and Buzz's stories, which were also independent, support and even extend Peewee's experiences. Can this really be mass hallucination over many years?

It seems unlikely.

Since there is such firm corroboration of the strange events in Peewee's hostelry, it seems natural to wonder what has been going on. Possibly the fact that the property is on part of the site of Trowbridge Castle has much to do with it. The castle was originally laid out in the twelfth century and developed during the later Middle Ages. Archaeologists excavating the site in the 1980s, before The Shires Shopping Centre could be built, found evidence of many graves in this area which still contained skeletons. Apparently the cemetery, which had developed around the medieval castle's chapel, extended under the foundations of Peewee's building. Therefore those graves and skeletons had to remain in place, as they do to this very day. There are no definite answers, but an awareness of the long history of this site does encourage speculation.

There are several significant features in these opening accounts which will be followed up later. But now here are a few more first-hand stories where ordinary objects have behaved in extraordinary ways. The following three accounts are all concerned with the same building.

FRANCES

Bill and I came to Bradford on Avon about 1965. We had bought the place as a grocery shop and delicatessen, but Bill made it into something very special and we used to be called "the little Fortnum & Mason's." We lived above the shop for six years, and then moved to Wingfield, but we continued with the business and were there for about eighteen years.

It was mostly a Queen Anne building, but parts of it were from the fifteenth century. You got to that part through a little door off the landing which led to two tiny bedrooms in the roof. We made a playroom for the children there, but they didn't like being in there at all. They said it was 'creepy' and they always found it very cold.

When we first came to the place, one of our assistants told us that we had a ghost called 'Annie.' We didn't tell the children, ever, but they must have picked up on something to have such a sense of unease. At the time the children were seven, nine and eleven years-old. Janice, the seven year old, was very imaginative and she would wake up in the night and creep into bed with her nine year-old sister who would complain bitterly. Janice never knew *why* she was so frightened, but she was always disquieted and wasn't happy living there. She never showed such nervousness before and was fine again once we moved to Wingfield.

There were many strange happenings in the building. The shop always had things falling off the shelves for no reason; often in the morning, when we went to open up, there would be tins of food rolling about on the floor. In the living quarters, sometimes we would hear noises in the night, as if someone was walking along the landing. It was a very old house and my husband said it was the wood settling at night, but there was a lot of disturbance.

Nothing that happened there was harmful or destructive, except for the night of water. We were all sound asleep but I'm a light sleeper and I woke to the sound of running water. At first I couldn't tell what was happening or where all the water was coming from. I went to the top of the stairs and it was pouring down the staircase. I ran downstairs and found that the sitting room was flooded with about two inches of water and it was pouring from the centre light, which was underneath the bathroom.

I ran up and down the stairs a couple of times – *quite* hysterical – then I ran into the bathroom. The previous owners had had a wash basin and taps installed in a cupboard in there to use for filling buckets for cleaning. We had *never* used these taps but here was one of them turned full on with water absolutely streaming out of it. The tap was extremely stiff and I had great difficulty when I tried to turn it off.

Bill said, "Oh, there must be some logical explanation for it." He tried to say that, a long time ago, the tap must have been left on, that no water had come out and then pressure had built up and it had come on by itself. But I can't really believe it happened that way, not after we'd been there for almost six years.

The people who owned the place before us were only there for two years but, according to one of our assistants, the couple before them had been there for a long time. In 1983, we sold to a young couple who tried to carry on the shop as we had had it, but they didn't make a success of it. Since then, many different businesses have occupied those premises and I hope Annie isn't causing the present owners any trouble.

SHAUN L.

I'm a country man, me. I've been a gamekeeper and I used to do a bit of poaching when I was a youngster; it takes one to catch one, like. I've been all through the woods in these parts, all around Iford and Freshford and up through Hinton Charterhouse. I've walked between the trees alone in the early hours of the morning and the dead of night when it's windy and dark, so I'm not exactly scared of my own shadow and I'm not afraid of bumps in the night.

Back in 1982 I was living with a young lady here in Bradford on Avon. We were in our early twenties and liked to enjoy ourselves; on the week-ends we'd go around the town, stopping in at the local delicatessens and other nice food shops.

One Saturday morning, we went into a shop on Silver Street and were chatting about what we might fancy for lunch when suddenly a tin – about the size of a tin of tuna or salmon – flew off a shelf and right across the room. We were dumbfounded and just stood there with our mouths open.

There were two ladies working behind the counter and one looked at the other and said: 'Oh, that's 'George' or 'Fred' – they gave it some sort of a name like that and I said, "Excuse me, would you like to explain who the hell George is? Tins don't just fly off the shelves by themselves." But they didn't tell us, so it remained a mystery. I don't remember whether we chose something for lunch or whether we were so shaken that we left without buying anything.

Eventually I forgot all about it but, almost twenty years later, I was working at Hilperton, helping a friend to trim some hedges. The house belonged to an old chap and his wife and after we'd been working there a while, he came out and asked if we'd like a cup of tea.

We got to chatting and when I told him we lived in Bradford on Avon, he said, "I used to live there."

"Oh, yeah, whereabouts, like?"

"Oh," he said, "it was above a food shop in Silver Street ."

I was going to blurt out the story of my visit there, but I stopped myself and said "I know it. Nice place to live, isn't it?"

"It was all right," he replied, "but it was a bit strange."

"What do you mean, strange?"

"Oh, things'd go missing and there'd be bumps and bangs during the night with things moving about unaccountably."

I told him what had happened to me that day, years ago, and again he said: "Oh, yes. It was a very strange place to live." When he said that, I had the same weird feeling that I did when I saw the tin fly off the shelf.

What I saw in that place wasn't natural and I remember how scared it made me. I *know* that tin didn't just fall off the shelf – it was thrown. I know it happened and so do the people who worked there.

JENNY G.

I worked at the Silver Street delicatessen for fifteen years and I believe the flat upstairs was haunted. Bill [the man in Shaun L's story] lived there at that time and things were always happening up there.

Down in the shop I never saw anything in particular, but we had a presence we called Annie in there and she was quite active. Things were always falling off the shelves – tins and packets of biscuits dropping to the floor.

We'd just laugh, pick them up and put them back on the shelf and say, "There goes Annie, up to her tricks again."

She never did any harm, although she startled a few people, but she was certainly very much a part of the shop.

Here are further examples of this type of activity.

ROB, chef at the Cross Guns

It's strange but I don't find the Cross Guns to be a frightening place, even with everything that happens here. Take the kitchen: there's hardly a day when something isn't moved or goes missing. I had a tub of red cabbage that I'd prepped and put in the fridge and then couldn't find it. I took every item out of that fridge and it wasn't there; I looked away and looked back and there it was sitting in the front of the fridge! Knives disappear and then turn up a week later in places where you'd never put a knife; lots of things go missing, food orders, plates, all sorts: something's going on that we can't explain and we're not mad people.

JUDITH

Things would go missing, as well, usually my knitting and needlework. I always kept it in a particular place, but when I'd go to get it, it would be gone. You could search the house through and never find it, but a few days later, there it would be in its original place.

ELIZABETH

A strange thing connected with my grandmother was the puzzle of the silver cross. It was Grandma's and Mum gave it to me. We went through several years of this cross disappearing and reappearing in the strangest places. The most bizarre time was when it had gone for some time only to be found in the fireplace of a house we'd just moved to. After a while we realised that although the disappearance of the cross didn't have any special cause or effect, when it re-appeared it was a sign of trouble to come. The cross has been gone for a long time now, and although part of me misses it, I know I'd be worried if Grandma suddenly sent it back again.

Another example, graphically and convincingly described, comes from Florence.

FLORENCE

"I'm going on up now to have me bath," I said to my husband, Ron.

I've always been a precise kind of person. I arranged my clothes on the bed, ready to put on and, as always, took off the cross and chain I wore and laid it on the bed – not just thrown down, but in a straight line.

When me bath was finished and I was dressed, I thought, "I'll go downstairs and make Ron and I a drink." But, when I got downstairs, I realised I'd forgotten to put on my cross. Back up I went to get it, but when I got to the bed, the cross was gone. "That's funny," I said to myself. Back downstairs I went and I said to Ron, "What have you done with my cross?"

"I haven't had your cross," our Ron said. Now, my husband was very, *very* staid – he wasn't one to play tricks and he didn't like anyone accusing him of anything that weren't right.

"Of course you have," I said. "I laid it out on the bed like I always do when I have me bath."

"I haven't had it," he said again. "Maybe it's on the floor."

Well, I trudged back upstairs and looked on the floor but it wasn't there. Down again I went. "Come on, our Ron, don't mess about. After all, you know I like me cross, so don't mess about."

"I'm *not* messing about and I don't like bein' accused of summat that I 'aven't done!"

"Well, that's bloomin' funny then – where's it gone to? Now – I *will* find it. If I have to strip the bed right off, I'll find it!" Up I went and stripped the bed clean but no cross came to light. I called down to my husband: "Can you come up and turn the mattress. It's stripped down and it'll save me doing it next time."

Ron came up and turned the mattress. I remade the bed and that was that, but all day I kept saying, "Well, it's bloomin' funny where my cross went to. I can't understand it. I *know* where I left it – on the bed like always – and it's completely *gone*!" My husband swore blind that I couldn't have done – that I must have put it somewhere else, but I was unshakeable.

The next morning I did my housework as always, laid my clean clothes on the bed like I did every day, went into the bathroom and had me wash, came out to dress and there was the cross and chain laid straight out on the bed, just as I'd left it the day before.

I called to Ron, "Come here and have a look at this! *What* do you make of that?"

"I expect it was caught in the bedclothes," he said.

"It couldn't have been. I stripped the bed bare. You *saw* – you even turned the mattress yourself. You can see how it's laid out – that's neat, not rumpled. If it had been caught in something, it wouldn't be laid out like that."

He had no answer and neither has anybody else – certainly not me.

Most of us have occasionally searched for items which have disappeared and reappear later, sometimes in a totally different place. Usually there is a rational explanation for these tiresome events, often in terms of human behaviour, such as forgetfulness or interference by another person. Looking for explanation elsewhere would, according to Piers Bizony, be 'the wrong kind of physics.' But these kinds of accounts, well authenticated, have come from many different sources where contributors are adamant that such strange movements of objects through time and space have occurred.

Dom Petitpierre, who was called in to help and advise in many case of violent occurrences and missing objects has no doubt that such events do take place and are not, necessarily, due to human causes. He gives such events the name of 'telekinesis' which is a Greek word meaning roughly 'energy applied from a distance'. This is a term normally used to classify the various aspects which make things move without applying physical energy.

He explains poltergeist activity as related to a specific person who has somehow, quite unwittingly, brought about the physical movement of objects. He goes on to say:

> I must emphasise that in all cases of poltergeist activity, those involved tend to be as baffled and frightened by the phenomena as everyone else.... Some people may provide a conduit for paranormal events while the vast majority never experience anything unusual.

Still focusing on physical evidence, here is Enid's account of one aspect of her early married life.

ENID

I've lived in Bradford on Avon all my life. I was born in Bridge Street, but a few years later my dad built a bungalow on the Winsley Road and I lived there with my parents until I got married.

Ken, my husband-to-be, had heard someone in the pub saying that Bertie Reynolds had bought a house on Newtown and that he was going to live in one half and let the other half out. So, one day, I saw Mr. Reynolds and I said, "I've heard you're renting your house out. Would you consider letting us have it," I said, "'cause Ken and I are planning to get married, but we don't want to set our date until we've got somewhere to stay."

So, he said, "Oh, ahh, I'll have a word with the Missus," and the Missus said, "Yes, all right." They used to live in Turleigh and they knew my father-in-law because he was the Co-op bread man for deliveries there, so Mr. Reynolds said "Yes, you can have it." So, we got married – that was in July of '51, – had the house for fifteen shillings a week and thought ourselves lucky to get it.

It was a very old house and it was built into one of the arches they have there. We had no water and no toilet – nothing like that. The loo was in a little walled garden, up some very steep steps and there was one cold water tap at the top. All the water had to be carried from there to the house and I used one of the little archways as a scullery. There wasn't a drain, but Ken stacked up stones and put an old sink on top and a big bin underneath; that was my washing up place and it saved me from walking up and down the steps time after time. In the evenings, Ken would empty the bin and I'd have it all ready again for the washing up water the next day.

It was hard work, especially when I was pregnant with Steve, but my mum used to let me come up to the bungalow and do the washing in her washing machine and dryer and that was a big help.

The house wasn't what I was used to because I'd come from a modern bungalow, but it was a place of our own where we could come and go as we pleased.

Things were always happening in that house. Sometimes you'd come home and though you knew you'd put the lights out when you left, they'd be on when you got back: you'd put something down, then go to get it later and it wouldn't be there and then you'd find it somewhere else.

We had doors with heavy metal latches that you had to press hard with your thumb to open, but they'd open on their own and you couldn't blame it on a draught because the house was sheltered from wind. Often, when we had friends in visiting, the door would open and I'd just get up and shut it. They'd all be so busy talking that nobody really noticed.

I always felt comfortable there, never frightened or intimidated – nothing like that, but Ken would never stay there on his own and when I was in hospital having the baby he stayed with his mother.

One Sunday, we went out to a race meeting, which we used to do most weekends and just before we left Ken said, "Make sure all the lights are out." I said, "I've been all over the house and they're all out." So, off we went. We spent the entire day at the race meeting and when we came back Ken said, "I told you to put the lights out before we left!"

"I did," I said.

"Well, the light at the bottom of the stairs is on."

"Well," I said, "I put it out!"

When you switch a light on and touch the bulb, it's hot. This light had a 100 watt bulb and it was switched on but when Ken touched it, it was stone cold, which was a puzzle.

I said to him again, "I switched it off." And he said, "Oh, never mind, then," but he went on about wasting money on the electric, like men do.

Ken was tired after the day out and said he was going to bed right after supper, so I got the food ready and we sat down at the dining room table but we didn't sit for long; while we were eating there was an awful noise, like a huge bang, upstairs in the bedroom.

"Whatever's that?" Ken said.

"Are there any windows open?" I asked. "'Could the cat have got in?"

We both went upstairs. The bedroom door was closed and when we opened it and went inside we saw that the window was shut and the cat wasn't there.

Our bed stood against the back wall and by the side of the bed, in a corner, we had a table with a bedside lamp on it, but the lamp wasn't on the table; it was lying in the middle of the floor with the cable stretched its full length, as if somebody had carefully placed it there.

I picked up the lamp and put it back on the table. We were a bit mystified but we went downstairs and finished our supper. After that I washed up and we went to bed.

We went to sleep easily enough but about two o'clock in the

morning we heard a huge crash up on the third floor. That was the attic and Ken had a workbench up there; he'd been tinkering with a motor bike engine and he'd left it on the bench.

We both sat bolt upright in bed. I switched on the light and we saw that the bed was covered in flakes of whitewash from the ceiling and flakes of it were still floating down.

"Good God," Ken said, "the engine's fallen off the bench!" So he goes upstairs but the engine was on the bench, there wasn't a tool out of place; everything was just as he'd left it and yet we'd heard this enormous bang from up there and these flakes of whitewash all over the bed and the floor.

Ken was really shaken by it – not at all happy, but for some reason it didn't bother me. As I said, I never felt menaced or threatened by anything that happened in that house, whether it was doors opening, or things disappearing or this terrible noise and the whitewash falling all over the place. But, as I said, Ken would never stay in the house on his own. I'd often be there alone with the baby as Ken was a driver with the Avon. He'd be away overnight many times but it never worried me.

The house had a long, stone archway at the bottom of the stairs and in the damp weather it was full of slugs, those horrible great big black ones. But they helped us in the end because when we put in for a council house, people from the Council came round to inspect where we were living. They saw me sweeping out those dreadful slugs and said "She can't live with a baby in a place like this!" We got our council house with no problem and we moved from Newtown on New Year's Day in '56.

You know, I wouldn't watch a horror film, not if you gave me fifty pounds – they frighten me to death and I won't watch anything spooky on the television, either. And yet, I was never ever frightened by that house. The things that went on there never caused any harm. They were just part of the place.

The appearance of whitewash flakes all over the bed is difficult to explain away – as is the cold electric light bulb which had been burning for many hours. Is it possible to explain these effects in terms of paranormal activity? Sudden cold or lights which behave in curious and illogical ways are so frequent in these stories that it would be very satisfying to be able to offer an explanation. Unfortunately this is not possible. Scientists are more likely to argue that when ordinary domestic items behave in a strange way, the explanation can be traced to faulty electrical wiring, the need for a new washer or airlocks in the plumbing.

Roger's experiences were dramatic. Whatever the causes, he has his own idea of why they happened.

ROGER

Until last year I worked at an automotive company which manufactured car parts. I enjoyed my job but I'm retired now and have had time to reflect on the strange events that happened there in the autumn of 2003.

I was one of a group of six people and we worked in an area known as a cell. My job mainly involved working three presses that manufactured engine mountings. About the end of October, strange things began happening in the cell. Several times a day, on the two to ten shift, water would be thrown at me from behind. At first I thought the others were fooling around and I got a bit rattled but it soon became apparent that nobody was doing it. It went on for about a month and once I even saw water spouting up from the floor and arcing to a height of seven feet before hitting me on the back of the neck.

In the early part of November I was doing some packing – putting engine mounts into boxes. The manufacturing process consisted of the parts being moulded, after which they'd go to the builder for assembly. Then they'd come through to me on a conveyor belt, ready to be packed. One day I went around to talk to the builder and on my way from the packing area I heard a rustling sound. When I returned to the packing area I felt something hit me on the back of the neck. I turned around to look and there on the floor were tiny fibre balls, about a quarter of an inch in diameter. A bag of these balls had been at the side of the building station and I realised that the rustling sound I'd heard was the balls leaving the bag, just before they were thrown at me.

On another occasion I was working on the bench with the presses. Adjacent to each press we kept the articles needed to load the presses. Items such as bolts and small colanders would be stacked six high, ready for loading. At least three or four times a day these would come flying down between the press and the bench and they'd hit the floor and scatter along the concrete. One time our team leader actually saw the colanders levitate before they fell to the ground.

There had been a young man working in the area just behind our cell. He'd been fired earlier in the year and it was believed that he'd been using drugs. He committed suicide in August and two months later all these strange happenings began. They started, as I said, in late October, 2003 and they ended in mid-November of that year. If it was his spirit causing mischief, evidently he felt he'd had enough revenge by that time.

The stories so far have focused on physical evidence. If objects hurtle through the air for no apparent reason, if possessions disappear, are searched for – often by several people – and then inexplicably reappear, if the contents of a room are physically rearranged, then surely it can be said that something has been *seen* to happen.

This group of stories all feature an interactive presence – something which is determined to be noticed. In Eleanor Macbeth's opinion, this is not always the case.

> What people call ghosts can simply be a memory pattern, a stored energy that is just repeating, like a looped film with no interaction between it and the observer. But you can get the type of entities that have consciousness and who interact. I think some of those are people who were alive on this earth but who, for some reason, can't move on.

Scientific analysis can take us even further, as Piers Bizony suggests:

> In technology, materials with memory are becoming more and more important; that's one area where science is perhaps surprising itself and there are many studies on that.
>
> There are materials where you take a spring-shaped object, for instance, or an object in the shape of a triangle; heat it and stamp it into a different shape – say a circle or a square – then, when you heat it again and let it relax, it'll go back to its original spring or triangle shape.
>
> There's a little work being done now in homoeopathy studies, on water seeming to retain the memory of substances that have been in it. There may or may not be something in that but there are a few experiments that are producing some interesting results.

Shaun Ogbourne also makes reference to information carried in water:

> In homoeopathy you can dilute a substance, whatever it might be, to such a degree that almost certainly no particle of that original substance is in the water, and yet the water will still carry the effects. The same thing happens with flows of underground water that can carry information and I think that there is a way there of enhancing telepathic contact in this manner.

CHILDREN & FAMILIES

Elizabeth – Kevin – Jade – Jackie – Sarah
Sue D – Ray – Alexander –Sophie Barnes – Ali
Angela – Elizabeth - David – Di – Dom Petitpierre

Children can take for granted all kinds of happenings which adults know cannot possibly be genuine, but perhaps young children have some kind of innocent entry into other layers of existence.

This first account comes from parents who thought their little boy was playing a childish game.

ELIZABETH

My daughter, Kirsty and her son, Jacob, were staying with us for a while. Jacob was about two and didn't speak very much at that point, but he kept going to the back of the sitting room and saying, "Hello, lady. Hello, lady." And he'd stay there, shaking his head or nodding – that sort of thing. He went on for weeks like this and Kirsty said, "I think he's gone nuts." We thought it must be an imaginary friend like children often have.

One day, the landlord came over and sat chatting with us. Jacob went across the room and started his usual "Hello, lady". The landlord looked at him and said to me, "Who's he talking to?"

"Oh," I said, "he's been doing this ever since he came. Every morning, the first thing he does is go over to the French doors and talk to the lady."

He looked at me for a minute and then said, "Will he understand if I tell you what I'm about to say?"

"I shouldn't think so," I replied.

"That window," he said, "was my mother's favourite spot in the house. She sat there, looking out, all day. Whenever I visited her, I always went to the French windows before I came in, so she'd know I was there. One day, I came up to the windows and she was dead in her chair. I think your grandson is seeing her spirit."

It is quite common for a child, especially one on his or her own, to create an imaginary friend as a companion and comforter. But the story which follows seems to be much more than that. Kevin's account takes us back to the days when the world was a safe enough place for parents to allow their children to wander off on their own.

KEVIN

I was born in Wiltshire, but was moved from there as a tiny child. When I was six years old, I was adopted and returned to the West Country. My adoptive parents lived in Bradford on Avon and I settled in to their home on the Trowbridge Road happily enough.

I was pretty much of a loner– didn't really mix well with other kids and even as a young child I used to go off on my own. One of my favourite pastimes was to walk around town, discovering the joys of Bradford on Avon and the best place of all was the Tithe Barn at Barton Grange Farm. Whatever my mood, whether

I was feeling down, lonely or happy, I'd go down to the Tithe Barn, which seemed to fill every need for me.

The cricket field wasn't far from the Barn; although I didn't play, I enjoyed watching it, but what I liked best to do was to go into the Tithe Barn with three little sticks and a ball. I'd put the sticks against the wall at one end of the Barn and I'd throw the ball at the sticks imagining myself as a famous cricketer. I never tired of this game, and I'd be at it at least twice a month.

When you enter the Tithe Barn by the main door, there's a door exactly opposite, but further along is another door and in the wall to the right of that door is an alcove. One day, as I was throwing the ball and running up and down, a figure emerged from the wall and stood in the alcove, watching me.

Now – before I saw him, I'd been talking out loud to myself, as kids do; I think I was unhappy or upset about something. I'd thrown the ball and it landed near where I'd set my wickets up and, as I went to get it, I felt that there was something there; I turned around and that's when I saw this apparition.

It was a young person, probably a teenage boy. He had on a tight-fitting hat with a turned up brim and a long point at the back of his neck; he wore a cloak and a knee-length tunic, all in a kind of greyish-brown hessian. He was barefoot and gaunt, a little drawn as if he hadn't been properly fed, and he seemed solid, like a real person. I asked him who he was and he didn't answer in words, but made an open armed gesture that seemed self-explanatory. I kept on playing – throwing the ball, then running and catching it on the rebound, all the time talking to him and getting these non-verbal responses that were comforting to me.

He stayed there for a long time, then he stepped back into the alcove and disappeared. I was sorry to see him leave but my thought after he'd gone was, "Oh, I've got a friend."

I played in the Tithe Barn many times; sometimes my friend appeared and sometimes he didn't and I was always disappointed when he wasn't there. When he did come, standing silently in his alcove, I chatted non stop, complaining when something was making me unhappy or giving him whatever good news I had to share. He always responded in the same silent way, with hand gestures and some almost telepathic kind of communication. Although I never heard a voice even inside my head, he always gave me an answer.

I saw my friend about five times over a two year period, when I was between six and eight years of age. He stopped coming a little later and I felt the loss of him quite keenly. I never thought of him as a ghost at that time and I never told anyone about him until many years later, when I realised that he couldn't have been of this world. I've never heard of anyone else seeing anything in the Tithe Barn, but I'd really like to know if anyone else has had a similar experience.

Kevin asks if anyone else has had a paranormal experience in Bradford on Avon's Tithe Barn. We await replies.

Several contributors have provided us with stories from their early days in other parts of the country and it would have been interesting to include some of these accounts. But, as this collection is limited to West Wiltshire, regretfully, they have had to be omitted. Jade, however, grew up in West Wiltshire and recounts two of her early childhood experiences.

JADE

When I was about six years-old I used to stay with my grandparents on Saturday nights. They lived in a building above a club on Market Street in Bradford on Avon. Their flat was quite high up from the street and I think they had three floors. You went through a door marked 'private' and there was a kind of half staircase with a room leading off that and then you went up the other half of the stairs to the rest of the flat. I used to sleep in the lower room because it was nice and cosy down there.

One Sunday morning, I was going to the room to get my things ready to go home. On the way downstairs there's a window – quite old-fashioned – with sort of half-see-through blinds. As I was going downstairs, I glanced at the window and saw some fingers. They began to come up on the outside of the window, behind the frame. I stopped and looked hard: a hand came up – it was very thin with long bones and it looked very delicate. It didn't exactly wave – more sort of swayed a bit and I became very, *very* frightened and I ran back upstairs, straight to my grandmother and told her what I'd seen. She 'there-there'd' me and said, "Don't worry, there's no silly ghost here."

What I'd seen was quite high up from the ground and you couldn't get to that window even with a ladder because there was a wall attached to the next building and only a tiny square of space. I was so young that I got over my fear quickly but, if I hadn't believed my grandmother, I think I'd have been afraid for quite a long time.

My mother and I moved to a cottage on the Bath road when I was about seven years old. We had the ground floor, with the sitting room and kitchen, the middle floor had my mother's bedroom, the bathroom and a spare room and then there was the attic and that's where I slept.

It was sometimes a bit eerie in the attic, especially if you're only seven or eight and I usually came down to the middle floor and got dressed for school in the spare room so that I could be close to my mother. I was getting dressed one morning and I was a little tired, but not sleepy, and I saw a very, *very* pale lady walk past the door quite slowly, towards the stairs. She looked quite a lot like my mum, so I thought that's who it was. But then I heard the hairdryer turn on in my mum's room so I knew it couldn't have been her.

I ran to my mother and told her what had happened. Although she "there, there'd" me a bit – like my grandma had done a few years back, I know she believes that I saw her.

JACKIE, Jade's mother

When we moved in to the cottage on Bath Road, I felt that there was somebody else there with the two of us – Jade and me. I sensed that it was a lady and that she wasn't very happy to have us there but, after a month or so, I felt that she had got used to us. I still felt her presence, but it wasn't frightening at all – it felt good. So I wasn't surprised when Jade told me about her experience. I'm sure it was the same lady and that Jade had actually seen her.

Next comes a pre-teenaged girl who went from being a non-believer to having total acceptance of, and considerable interaction with, the spirits she met in her new home.

SARAH

I was about twelve years-old when we moved to the house in Trowbridge, which was where all the events took place. I had never believed in anything supernatural, so my first experience was a real shock. It took place one evening when I was in bed, reading a *Jackie* comic magazine. I felt that somebody was watching me, so I looked up and saw a small boy at the end of my bed. He was very clear to me, quite solid looking. I'd say he was about nine years-old, blonde and wearing a brown jacket and trousers in the style of the Cavalier times. He had a sad, lonely expression on his face.

I ran out of the bedroom and down to my mother, shouting that there was a boy in my room. My mother said I looked as if I'd seen a ghost. I was terrified and wouldn't go back to the bedroom, which I shared with my sister, Julie, unless she went with me. When we went into the room, there was nobody there, but he visited me almost every day from then on. I called him Danny and I became quite used to having him around.

He often responded to my questions and when I asked about his parents, he brought his father to see me. He was a kind looking man with a round face and red cheeks – not much hair. He seemed very proud of Danny, standing behind him with his hand on his shoulder. Danny also showed me a picture of his mother; it was a miniature in a frame that he held in the palm of his hand. He never changed in all the times he came – always the same age, always in the same clothes, always with the sad look on his face. I've sometimes wondered if he's still there and if anyone who lives there now has seen him.

There was so much going on in that house – it was so *busy* all the time that it just became a way of life. If it wasn't Danny in the bedroom, it was people going up and down the stairs. There was a central staircase that branched off on either side and I'd often see something go past – sometimes a person, but often part of a cloak or a hat as if someone had just gone up and around a corner. Sometimes, I'd just hear them. I remember one afternoon, while I was doing my homework in the dining room, I thought my mother was coming down the stairs. She has a bad leg, which gives her a very distinctive sound when she's walking downstairs, heavier on one side than on the other. I expected her to come through the door from the stairs and instead she came via the kitchen, so it was someone else with a limp.

My mother had nicknames for the people I saw. One man she called Feather because he had a black hat with a red feather in it. He had a long face with sharp features. He wasn't frightening at all; in fact, I quite liked him. Another was known as George. He wasn't of the same era as Feather, who seemed to belong to the same time as Danny and his father. Then there was Sherlock – I called him that because he wore one of those capes. I think it was George who used to pull the duvet off my bed. At first I found it unnerving and sometimes I'd go upstairs and sleep with my brother, but then I got used to it.

So many things happened so often that one of my aunts said we should talk to them and say that they can't just wander around any time, waking me up in the middle of the night when I have school the next day, but that they could come at a specific time. So, we decided that Sunday mornings would be good; and my mum and I would sit in the dining room and she'd hear something and say "over in that corner", or wherever, and I'd look and see somebody. We weren't testing each other, but it was almost like a game...Feather...George...Sherlock.

In the end, there was so much going on that we got used to it and it was as if they were going about their everyday lives and so were we.

Sarah's story recounted many meetings with the beings who shared her house. She had much in common with Sue D., even though Sue's visitation was a one-time sighting.

SUE D.

My one and only experience of seeing a ghost was in the house in St. Margaret's Street which was where I lived from the age of five. At the time of the sighting I was about thirteen or fourteen. I remember that it was a Sunday morning;

I also recall that I was wearing a brand new Laura Ashley dress and I was very proud of it. I was doing the usual things that teenagers do in their bedrooms... a little homework... sorting things... pottering about, basically.

At the far end of my bedroom I had a large Victorian type wardrobe with a drawer underneath. I had been trying on clothes and the wardrobe door was open. I turned around and looked at the wardrobe and there, standing inside it, was a young boy around eight or nine years-old.

The most striking thing about him was his eyes – very big – *huge* brown eyes that were quite glassy looking. His face had the roundness of a young child, but his body was slight. He wasn't a ragged boy – didn't have raggedy clothes – in fact, he looked quite smart, but not *over* smart. He had dark hair and wore a dark tweed cap. His jacket was dark, too, and he had a light coloured shirt underneath it. Even though he was standing, I only clearly remember the top half of him. He had something of the look of a street urchin and I think he was from some time at the beginning of the last century. He held something in his hand – a towel or cloth of some kind – I'm not sure what.

We looked at each other for what seemed like a long time. His facial expression was one of melancholy and it didn't change at all. I hadn't felt any fear at all when I first saw him, nor did I as we continued to stare at each other; in fact, it seemed almost normal. After a little while, I sat on my bed, still looking at him and then I decided to shut the wardrobe door. It wasn't that I didn't want to see him any more but I wanted to see what would happen if he would push the door open or something. So, I closed the door and waited for a minute or two. Nothing happened. I opened the door again and he was gone.

I told my mum about it. First of all she thought I was talking about the type of ghost in a sheet – that sort of thing – but when I described it, she seemed quite receptive and came in my room to look. I suppose at first she did think, "perhaps she imagined it", but then she seemed to accept that I *had* seen it –

seen *him*, I should say. I'm sure she had heard other stories of things like this about other people and I think she tried to reassure me, to make sure I wasn't going to get worried about it.

For some time afterwards, I thought I would see him again. It didn't bring me any fear – like "Oh, I can't go to sleep", or "I can't open the wardrobe door". I did kind of worry about *him*, though, but I never did see him again. I had it in my head that his name was Jack and that's how I've always thought of him.

I left the house when I married but five years ago my husband and I moved back to look after Mum who had become chronically ill. I hadn't thought about it until recently but, interestingly, the room I saw Jack in was the newest part of the house. I use it now as my study. It had been built into the garden, a short time after the war and I've since heard that alterations to houses sometimes cause sightings like the one I had.

My grandmother was still living when I saw Jack. She was very, very superstitious – wouldn't stay in a room where there were thirteen people – was terrified if anything fell off the wall because it signified death – all that kind of thing and my mother warned me about saying a word to her. "Don't tell your Nan," she said – and I didn't.

And now to Ray's story. This event took place long ago, yet it had a repercussion in later years.

RAY

I was a young lad, about eleven or twelve years-old, when this happened to me.

It was a lovely summer's eve and my friend Sam and I were

out on Indigo Lane in Westbury. There used to be a silk factory there but now there's a tennis court, in front of the Matravers School.

In those days there was a stream on that land; it's probably been diverted since all the building that went on over there but, back then, the stream ran through an immense, thick wood and there was an old, rambling house owned by a French lady, Mrs. Breton. There were otters in the stream and she had built a dam of sandbags which created a pool for them to swim in. Like most boys, we were a little bit mischievous so we decided to move the sandbags off, just to see the effect of the water cascading over the top.

Like I said, it was a beautiful evening and, although it was around nine o'clock, there was still lots of daylight. While we were removing the sandbags, we stood back from the stream to see what progress we'd made and, as I looked to the other side, which was all dense forest, I saw a face – someone was looking at me. It was as solid as any human being, a male figure wearing a tricorn hat and a long, flaring black cloak. I could see its eyes very clearly – they glared straight at me, but I couldn't see anything of the face from the nose down and even in my terrified state I found that very strange. Terrified? – I was literally petrified. I simply could *not* move. Sam saw the figure too but after a couple of seconds he was able to cut and run. Not me – I was still glued to the spot. I stood there, mesmerised for what seemed like forever, even though it was probably only about thirty seconds. Eventually I managed to break free and I ran straight home and told my mother what had happened.

Many years later my daughter, who went to the Matravers School, brought home a library book.

"Dad," she said, "there's a lot of ghosts around Wiltshire, isn't there?"

"Yes," I said, "and I've seen one of them."

"Well, there's one in this book from around here."

"Don't show me," I said. "I'll show you what I saw."

I drew a picture of what I'd seen and while I was drawing, it was as if I was back there, seeing the eyes glaring at me again. After I finished my picture, my daughter opened the book and there on the page was the identical figure to the one I'd drawn.

I have since found out that there was a highwayman called Thomas Boultier in this area. He terrorised the people in these parts for quite some time but eventually he was caught and hanged. I could never understand why I didn't see all of his face but the picture in the book showed that the lower half of his face was covered by a handkerchief.

What Sam and I had seen as boys was confirmed thirty-five years later by the book my daughter brought home. Poor Sam is gone now, but he'd be glad to know that what we saw wasn't imaginary – we saw it clear enough. Fifty-eight years have passed since that night at the stream but I remember it plain as can be to this day.

Ray's strong visual recall, so many years later, shows just how vivid his experience was for him. This encounter was never repeated. However his grandson, Alexander, seems to have a much closer engagement with another world, or worlds, which continues.

ALEXANDER

I didn't know that most people couldn't see the things that I see – it all seemed natural to me, from the time that I was very little.

The first thing I remember happening was when I was two years-old and the plates went flying. My mum was at work and my grandad and I were in the kitchen. The plates were in the dish rack on the counter and they just flew up over me. I put my hands over my head, but they didn't hurt me. They all landed on the stone floor and none of them broke.

When I was three, my Mum's Nan tickled me on the back of my neck. Mum was in the bath and I was standing near the bathtub, looking the other way, when my neck was tickled. I don't know why, but I had an idea it was Mum's Nan and then Mum told me it was her, because she used to see her. It only happened to me once or twice.

The person I saw most often was my Grandad Ian. I don't remember him, because he died when I was two, but I saw him in my old bedroom when I was about five. It was like he was laying down with a big light shining on him and I could see him on the wall.

The next time was the day before we went on holiday. Grandad Ian came to my bedroom and told me that while I was away on holiday he was going to play on my computer.

Our toilet was downstairs and if I came down to use it, Grandad always followed me down the stairs. He was just a black figure, sort of solid, but I could see part of his face – his beard and glasses, anyway. It happened almost every day, but when we moved he just sort of stopped coming.

One day, when Mum and I were in the car, travelling back to Westbury, I saw a figure in the back seat by the door. He looked like a shadow, but I could see his hat and his pipe and he had a walking stick, too. I was sitting in the front and he put his hand out towards me. He was there for about three minutes and then he disappeared. I didn't say anything to Mum until we got to Grandad's, and when I described him, she showed me a photo and it was her Grampy.

But sometimes I've seen people who aren't members of my family. When I was in the living room watching telly, there were two people in there fighting, with shields and swords. The figures were black like shadows, but the weapons looked solid. They didn't make any sound and I just carried on watching telly and let them fight.

The last thing I saw was in the bedroom of my new house: it was a boy, about nine or ten and he appeared suddenly, standing on my bed. He had dark hair and he was dressed in ordinary clothes. He didn't look at me – he was staring out of the window, which is behind my bed. He just stood there for a minute or two and then he disappeared and I haven't seen him since.

I know, now, that most people don't see these things but it still seems quite normal to me.

Sophie Barnes, who is a healer and very aware of other worlds, makes the following comments:

> I think, very often, young children see things, especially very young children and it's programmed out of them, rather, because people don't believe them. So they learn that it isn't sensible to say that there's a little boy out in the garden or whatever, but a lot of little children do have imaginary friends. Alexander seems to be clairvoyant. He remains very calm about strange events, such as people fighting in the living room, because if you are aware that there is an alternative reality, if that's what you've always known, it doesn't scare you.
>
> It sounds as though Alexander sees things more solidly than I do. I don't know quite what the word would be. But, for example, I think when people die, often their nearest and dearest continue to see them around. It's passed off as hallucination, but for them it isn't like that at all. They cope because they feel strongly that the dead person is still with them. Certainly this has happened to friends of mine.
>
> For a long time in my life my experience was that it simply was not safe to say any of the things I saw

> because some people would think I was weird. The difference is that now I move in very different circles. A lot of my friends are healers and this sort of thing is just completely taken for granted. A lot of people have had this experience."

Research for this book has included discussion with several clairvoyants who support Sophie's comments. Invariably they have been aware of figures from other worlds from an early age, taking such companions for granted and gradually realising that most people do not share these experiences. Clairvoyancy is often not taken very seriously by the everyday world. But Alexander's story and others suggest that these worlds are open to some human beings although not to everyone.

Such awareness can be more easily understood by considering the faculty of hearing. Some people's hearing is much better than others. Some can hear a very high frequency, while others cannot hear it at all. Some are blessed with perfect pitch, most of us are not.

Sound waves are only one way in which we receive energy through the ether. Possibly awareness of other worlds is a similarly variable ability. It can be argued that virtually all of us, except some gifted few of the population, cannot get beyond the one world we inhabit, while people like Alexander and Sophie have some sort of extra-sensory perception, almost a sixth sense of the universe and its potentials.

Many psychics would say that family members, now dead, may try to reach us from 'the other side'. Without getting too far into these matters, here are some stories which seem to bear out such statements.

ALI

My family has been in Bradford on Avon since at least the seventeen hundreds. My paternal grandmother, whom this story is about, was born into our working class family at the end of the nineteenth century. She grew up here and, when she became a young woman, she went to London to go into service in one of the big houses.

She returned here to marry and brought with her a Victorian swing mirror, which was probably given to her as a wedding gift by her employers. The mirror was with her for the rest of her life and, when she died, it went to my father.

My grandparents were unusual people for their time. They were anti-religion – didn't believe in church; in fact, they thought the church did harm – and my grandfather, unlike most men of the Victorian era, played with his children and spent a lot of time with them.

When I was small, Gran lived with us for a year and she'd often put us to bed and when we were settled for the night she'd sit at the end of the bed and sing or tell us stories. She and I had a close relationship but not a traditional 'Granny and child' one. She'd talk to me in a way that sometimes caused my parents to say: "Ooo, Mum – that's a bit much!" But she still spoke to me about everything, even about dying which I found distressing at the time but now I'm glad that she did.

In the summer that I was ten, Gran was visiting my aunt in Weston-Super-Mare. We were going to pick her up, which was very exciting because it meant we would spend the day on the sea front. But when I woke up that morning I knew something had changed, *really* changed and I was dragging my heels about getting ready. My parents were chivvying me: "Hurry up – hurry up and get washed and dressed." I said: "We're not going to Weston-Super-Mare today," and my parents said: "Well, of *course* we are, we're going to pick your grandmother up." Well, clearly I couldn't say "She's not coming home." But I knew, I just *knew* that I wasn't going to meet her that day.

We didn't have a telephone, not many people did in those days; a knock came at the door and there stood the police – that was the way messages got across – and the next thing I knew we were grieving at the news that my grandmother had died that morning.

I missed her a lot and I remember one morning as a teenager waking up and feeling grief again that she'd gone because in the moment I awoke, it was almost like she was alive – a second when I thought, "Oh, Gran's here – Gran's staying." And perhaps that happened after one of the first times she came to me. She's come like that at least half a dozen times since she died. I used to think of it as a dream, but now I'm not so sure.

She sits on the bed, like she did when she lived with us, and she talks to me just like she used to, offering opinions and giving advice. She's in a simple blue dress – she always wore blue – and a knitted jacket, which is how I remembered her when I was a child. Her most striking features were her dark hair, which never went grey, even though she was seventy-eight when she died, and her lips. Gran always said she never had to wear lipstick because her lips were naturally red and when I see her, it's those features that stand out the most. Any other time I can only remember her shape and recall her scent, which was 4711 cologne. I smell it after all of her visits and even though you can still buy it I'd never want to wear it myself – it's her smell and I'll always associate it with her.

As a child I didn't realise just how closely I was linked to Gran; looking back, it was much closer than I knew and when I was growing up one of my biggest sorrows was that she wasn't here to share my experiences. When she began visiting me, I found that her advice often gave me a direction to go in; for instance, my husband is younger than me and when we met there were several people who threw that into the equation. We had begun thinking about making a commitment and, soon after that, Gran showed up at the end of my bed and said: "Oh, yes. He's a very nice man." It reassured me.

But I don't only see Gran at the end of my bed. When I became an adult, her mirror was given to me and I keep it on a chest of drawers in my bedroom. Over the years there are occasions when I see my grandmother's image in the mirror. Again, it's the image I would have had of her as a child. She doesn't speak – she doesn't move – she's there for just a few seconds, smiling at me and then she's gone. It's happened about a dozen times in the twenty-two years I've had the mirror, but that's enough times for me to expect it to happen again, even though I don't know when. I think it coincides with times when I'm in a reflective mood, I don't mean to make a pun but that's the best way of describing it, times when I'm thinking of all sorts of things – mostly family and which direction I'm going.

As I grew up and had the usual memorable occasions – getting married, having children – one of my biggest regrets was that Gran wasn't there to share them with me. I'd think: "I wish Granny was here: I wish she could see this." When my son, Jacob, was born, everybody came to see him and admire him, but the person I'd have liked most to come couldn't be there. But when he was about a year old, she did come and she said he was just like some member of the family – I can't remember which one she said. And then she told me something that gave me great joy. She said, "I sing to him, you know."

Of course, Jacob was too young to remember that and he's never reported seeing her. Nobody has ever seen her but me, neither in the mirror nor on the bed, but my husband believes in her appearances.

I believe that some people need to make a connection to the important people in their lives, even when those people are no longer of this world. My favourite auntie lived in the house that my grandmother died in and she was somebody I'd like to share things with. It's not that I talk to Gran as such, when she's not with me, but the other day I was thinking aloud and I said:

"Perhaps you could bring Audrey with you the next time you come."

I do like the idea of people being reunited, even though I'm not sure it's possible and it would be lovely to see my Auntie Audrey again but, whether or not she comes, I still have my visits from Gran and I'm happy that she's still a part of my life.

Ali's close relationship with her grandmother continues to this day.

Angela's story is particularly interesting because it caused her family to take action and the result was memorable.

ANGELA

For many years my grandparents had a lady living with them and when, several years ago, they passed away, she stayed on in their bungalow. Eventually, she decided to move to sheltered accommodation and my father and his sister and brother arranged to go and clean the house out.

The previous day, the kettle switched on and boiled itself for no apparent reason; the night before the cleaning day, my sister was awakened by an alarm clock that went off in the middle of the night, even though it hadn't been set and my father's watch, which had various wake-up calls on it, including a cockerel crow, also went off, unset, at an ungodly hour.

That particular evening, I went to bed as usual and at about three o'clock in the morning I heard this voice saying very sternly, "No one's listening to me – just *nobody* is listening to me." It was my grandmother's voice. I sat bolt upright in bed and said, "Nan, I'm listening to you. Whatever's the matter?"

I could see her in front of me, with my grandfather stood

behind her left shoulder. He was very quiet and didn't have a word to say.

"Alfie's tools," she said, "Alfie's tools!" Alfie was my grandfather's name.

I said, "What about Alfie's tools?"

"Don't get rid of Alfie's tools. He's very fond of them. You mustn't get rid of his tools!"

"Okay, fine," I said. "Please tell me where they are."

She described them in this particular shed. I had no knowledge of these tools, which she said were in a red metal box, but I promised her they'd be safe. "Don't worry about it," I said, "I'll sort it out." And I went back to sleep.

When I woke up the next morning I thought, "Did I dream it? Did I see it? What?" I drove to my mum and dad's and the nearer I got to their house, the more upset I became. I thought, "I've got to do something about it – I can't keep quiet, I must say what happened."

I ran up the path in tears and I said to my dad, "When you clear out the bungalow, please don't get rid of the tools. Nan's going to be really upset." I was quite distraught by this time and Dad said, "Okay, hang on – hang on. Tell me what's the matter."

I told him what happened and he said, "Fair enough. We'll see if they're there and I promise you we won't get rid of them." He went to the bungalow that day and, sure enough, there they were in the red box, in exactly the place she had described.

Nan's visit was a strange experience. I remember quite clearly that she was very solid looking, even though I only saw her from the shoulders up and my grandfather in the background, behind her. Although I've had experiences of her being with me, like her touching me on the neck, this was the only time I actually saw her. I wasn't frightened, but I was distressed because she was upset over the possibility of the tools being sold or given away and I was also worried that nobody would believe me. But they did and we have the tools to this day.

In this next account, Elizabeth describes some of her experiences. Her husband, David, was inclined to dismiss them, until he had an encounter of his own.

ELIZABETH

My grandfather was an engine driver; he died at the age of forty-six – far too young. He and my grandmother lived in Westbury and their house was a long way from the engine sheds, so my widowed grandmother had a house built close to the sheds as the engineers needed a place to stay overnight on what was called 'double home journeys'. They said they would guarantee her enough customers to repay the building loan and they were as good as their word; the loan was fully paid up – ahead of time. This gave my grandmother a steady income, so the house was very, very important to her. It was built in 1937 and, strangely, was started on her birthday and completed on mine.

Nan's name was Lillian and she died when I was eighteen months-old. I was around nine years old when peculiar things began to happen. When my bedroom door was open I could see out to the landing and to the bathroom door. One night I saw my mum walk through to the bathroom. I called to her twice, but she didn't answer and the next thing I knew it was morning, so I must have suddenly gone to sleep.

When I went downstairs, I said, "I saw you last night, Mum, and you didn't talk to me when I shouted to you."

"When did you shout to me?" she asked.

"When you went to the bathroom."

"I didn't go to the bathroom last night."

"Yes, you did. You were wearing that nice dressing gown."

"What dressing gown do you mean?"

I described it and Mum shot a look at my Dad, then she said,

"Yes. Yes, I did."

That was the end of the discussion and I didn't think anything more about it.

Many years later, I became interested in antique clothes and Mum said, "I've got some things upstairs in the wardrobe. You can have anything that you like from up there."

We went through all kinds of clothes, then – there was the dressing gown. I'd totally forgotten about it, but as soon as I saw it, I said to Mum, "That's the dressing gown!"

"What dressing gown?" she said.

I reminded her of the time I'd seen her in it.

"Oh, yes," she said, "but that dressing gown isn't mine. it was my mother's and I've never worn it."

I had only been around nine years-old when I first saw it, and now I just stood there, thinking, "What was it I saw back then?"

At around the same time in my childhood I'd laid down to go to sleep one night and once my head was on the pillow I heard the most dreadful gasping breaths. I sat up and it stopped but when I lay back down, it began again. I remember getting out of bed, pinching my arm and thinking "Am I awake?"

I thought, well, perhaps it's my brothers snoring, so I went to their room, but they were both still awake. Dad was working nights, so only my mother was home with us. I went back to bed, thinking that maybe I'd been dreaming but, when I put my head down to sleep, this terrible breathing started again – like someone struggling for air – it was awful. I ended up going into my mother's bed and she said I'd just had a bad dream.

Several years later, I found out that my grandmother was a dreadful asthmatic. Mum said it was so bad that when she had a severe attack they could hear her from downstairs. When she told me that I'd had a bad dream I could tell that she was covering up, like with the dressing gown, and I was always afraid when I went into that bedroom.

Those were *my* experiences with my grandmother, but my husband David had an encounter as well, much more recently.

DAVID

I've always been extremely sceptical. I've heard these stories from Tiz (Elizabeth) for many years and I tended to be like, "Yeah – right."

Four years ago we were living in Milton Keynes and we used to come down to West Wiltshire for a weekend every fortnight, staying part with Tiz's Mum, Jin, and part with mine. Tiz's parents had always used the front bedroom, but after her husband died, Jin moved to a room at the back where she felt more secure and the front room was kept for guests. The layout of the upstairs was such that if the bathroom door was open, you could see both bedroom doors. In the front bedroom, the bed faced the window and the door was behind you so you couldn't see who was coming into the room until the door was more than halfway open.

I got on well with Jin and every Sunday morning that we were there she'd have a cigarette in bed and then get up and bring tea to Tiz and me.

This incident happened just a fortnight before Jin died. On this particular Sunday morning, I woke up about seven o'clock and discovered that Tiz had got up and gone to the bathroom. It was just starting to get light outside and I lay there and thought, well, when she gets back, I'll go and have a leak.

I was conscious that the door had swung open and when it got past that halfway point, I could see that my mother-in-law had come part way into the room. She was a very little lady, only five foot two, very thin and with brown hair. She came in and looked straight ahead at the window where the curtains were still drawn. I said, "Hello, Jin," but she didn't answer and went back out again.

Tiz was in the bathroom with the door open and when she came back I said to her, "Is your Mum all right?"

"She's not up," she replied.

"Yes, she is. She's just been in, but she didn't speak."

Tiz shouted to her Mum through her bedroom door: "You okay in there?"

"Yes," she replied, "I'm just having a cigarette – why, is Dave waiting for his cup of tea, then? He'll have to wait till I've had my fag."

Tiz said to her, "Haven't you just been in, then?" and she said, "No, I'm not up yet, definitely."

I didn't believe it and I says to Tiz, "You're having me on, right?"

"No," she said, "*no*, she's in the bedroom still. *Nobody* has gone from that room to this, I've seen *nobody*. It's light enough to see; if she'd gone across to our room, I'd have seen her."

I couldn't believe it when Tiz said her mother hadn't been in but, of course, she would have seen Jin go across to the room and back. I can't remember whether she turned and left or if she backed out. Either way, at some point I would have seen her face – but I didn't. I mulled it over for weeks and weeks. I thought and thought and *thought* and I could *not* remember seeing her face. And that left the question – who *did* I see?

I never believed in any of this stuff, but the more I thought about this thing that happened, the more I thought there was something strange about it.

Jin, Tiz's mother, was five foot two and a half and weighed eight stone and Tiz's grandmother, Lil, was five foot two and weighed eight stone, so they were identically built. Jin died a fortnight after this happened and, as Tiz said when we talked about it, it must have been Lil, gone to the bedroom where Jin used to sleep. We can't think of any other explanation.

I was shaken up for the rest of the weekend, I really was. I've always been very sceptical about Tiz's experiences and I've had trouble accepting that this has happened to me...and now I'm beginning to think – has everybody got these stories...?

Unlike David, Di has always been sensitive to the spirit world. So the experience which she relates here seemed quite natural to her.

Di

As a nurse there have been many times that I've been with people when they died and I always had a strong feeling that their essence, if you like, had gone. The shell was left, but whatever was 'them', had definitely moved on. I was often aware of their spirits afterwards and sometimes I've seen them, too.

My mother-in-law had suffered with a bad heart for years. She was 82 years-old and had six children who wouldn't let her go. She said to me, "You know, I'm really, really ready to go. I really have had enough."

I was up at the Bradford on Avon market and I was suddenly aware of her smiling at me; I hadn't been thinking of her at that moment. It was November and I bought winter pansies, partly in memory but partly in celebration because she was obviously so relieved to have gone. She was being looked after at home. The whole family were very dependent on her and wanted her with them, but they'd taken her into hospital for respite care. She was having terrible difficulty breathing and she was absolutely ready to go. She was only in hospital for two hours when she died and they were all flabbergasted: "How terrible, being there just two hours and then she died." But I knew that as soon as she got away from them, as soon as they'd stopped holding her back – she'd be off. She was a very spiritual woman: she knew where she was going, she'd had enough, she wanted to go and she went.

What people actually *see* when they 'see a ghost' is a matter of strong dispute. Richard Gregory, a leading authority on perception, the psychology of seeing, would say that the brain is quite capable of creating ghosts by adopting strategies to make sense of what the eye sees.

Each person's perception is unique, a fact amply demonstrated in courts of law where, in all honesty, eye witnesses will present conflicting versions of the same event.

Many of us may not know whether or not we are psychically aware. As Dom Petitpierre says:

> Psychic awareness is not an easy thing to describe to anyone who has not experienced it. Fundamentally, it is a matter of information reaching one through the unconscious mind. When this information reaches the unconscious, it tends to get clothed in the easiest or most facile form. .... One person, therefore, might visualise the impression and 'see' a ghost! Another might hear something – a groaning sound, a clanking of chains and so on, or mysterious bumps in the night. Others might smell something. Some might combine the lot. Many of us, however, who are psychically aware, do not need to 'translate' the information in any way. The message itself comes into our minds and so we have no need to 'see' or 'hear'.

PERCEPTION

> We're just temporary assemblages of matter – of atoms, yet the stuff in our bodies has been around since the universe has been born and will be around until it dies. But we're only here for a very brief time. We're almost like telephone calls, temporary little buzzings in wires, then God puts the receiver down, and we're gone. We could become a few atoms in a flower, in the lungs of a cow, in the heart of a newly-formed sun: it's our matter and energy, but it's distributed in different forms.
>
> *Piers Bizony*

This seems an appropriate place to touch upon the compli cated subject of perception and how it can pertain to the sighting of ghosts.

The ways in which the eye receives stimuli and transmits this information to the brain, is an involved, highly complicated process. The retina, for example, has a hundred and twenty million receptors, like tiny photoelectric cells, which accept protons and then produce signals. These receptors funnel down to one million channels and then go to different regions in the brain, which adds its own information. This massive yet minute analytical process is done at extraordinary speed, yet we take it for granted in our daily lives and scarcely know that it is happening.

It is difficult for the mind to hold more than one vision of the same object or scene at the same moment. Take a minute to look at the three pictures opposite. Each one has two equally valid interpretations. Interestingly some people will see only one version of the picture and some will see just the second version. There are others who will recognise both interpretations but it is hard to see both at the same time.

REFRAINS & DISTURBED PLACES

Piers Bizony – Jean – Hilary – Julie – Mark – Sue W.
Dom Petitpierre - Martin – Sue S. – Piers Bizony

By now it is becoming clear that whatever walk of life contributors come from and whatever age they are, certain comments tend to recur. These could be called 'refrains', i.e. similar responses to manifestations which cannot be explained in rational terms, summarised here as: a previous disbelief in ghosts; a vivid recall of the event; a desire to keep the experience to oneself.

People comment on a drop in temperature or an intense cold which occurred at the time. This is a well known feature of ghost stories from Shakespeare to Stephen King and it is interesting to have first hand experiences which so frequently make the same point.

What causes this chill? Theories abound, one of which is that energy, which is highly complex and mysterious, has to be drained from the surroundings to enable the manifestation to occur. The word 'energy' has no simple explanation and it carries very different meanings to different people and can be used in many ways. Yogis work through chakras and invisible energy channels; acupuncture and reflexology, recognised holistic treatments, are also based on similar energy channels which course through the body.

We all take for granted the remarkable way in which technology has harnessed energy. E-mails are electro-magnetic waves which are transmitted across the world in nanoseconds, forming into messages only when we decide to open them. If harnessed cosmic energy can produce such results, it seems more than possible that there are other ways in which energy, perhaps from past centuries, can reappear.

Scientists are not happy about such speculations, as Piers Bizony explains:

> Science likes to deal with measurable, repeatable things but we can't be absolutely sure that the whole of human experience and cosmic activity is built out of these things. Science is very bad with anecdotal evidence; someone says: "I saw a ghost." And a scientist says: "Can I repeat the experiment? Can we sit here and see the ghost?" The ghost doesn't turn up and the scientist says: "Oh, you probably imagined it."
>
> So I can only state the outreaches of where science is and what it can speculate on, based on its need for repetition; for one person to make an experiment and another person to verify that experiment by doing the same thing and getting the same results. Classically, this is not what happens with ghosts.

Scientists look for proof but anyone, faced with curious situations, naturally has to deal with them in some way or another. One solution seems to be through giving a strange presence a name, thus bringing it into the family. It is rather like trying to come to terms with some troublesome physical complaint: once named it seems more under control.

Willow Cottage was home to several presences to whom the family gave names.

JEAN

Some of the happenings in Willow Cottage were disturbing, but not really frightening. My husband experienced some of the activities there. In fact, he once saw a group of soldiers, just from the waist up, at the back of the house; probably the height of the ground has changed from that time. It was supposed to be the area of the battle of Ethandun and the fields are still in front of Willow Cottage to this day.

My father was a total non-believer – he pooh-poohed everything we told him, but one day he came up the drive in his car and when he came into the kitchen he said, "I waved to Jason, he was in the garage." And with that, Jason came into the kitchen from upstairs. My father's face was a picture but he didn't say anything. It must have been our ghost, Danny, up there – he was the same age and appearance as Jason. There were shrubs and trees around the garage which would have hidden Danny's clothing and Dad just assumed it was his grandson.

The only time I actually saw anything was going upstairs to my bedroom. As I came out of my bedroom door, I could see across to the other set of stairs and just as I looked I saw a figure in a heavy, blue-grey hooded cloak that swung into the girls' bedroom.

I used to smell things, very strong odours. Once it was an overpowering smell of freesias but often it was snuff, which we associated with an apparition my daughter Sarah called Sherlock because, she said, "He's tall, Mummy and he wears a long, dark coat like Sherlock Holmes."

He wasn't particularly nice and he was usually in the kitchen area. Once I was in the kitchen, cooking, and I was wearing one of those cheesecloth shirts that were popular in the seventies. Just as I was putting the joint in the oven, my shirt was pulled out – away from my body, first on one side and then the other. Both Sarah and my husband saw it. I had to run out into the garden to get the teasing to stop. I used to get poked, too, the feeling of two fingers in my back was very definite, but that usually happened upstairs in my bedroom.

My husband was away a lot in those days and the footsteps going up and downstairs alarmed me at first, but for the most part we lived quite happily with it.

In the eighties we sold the house, to a couple with two young children. We went back to see how they had settled and the woman said, "I like the house because there's a presence here."

I think the place has been sold twice since then and I often wonder if things are still going on there.

"Teasing" is an interesting word for Jean to use to describe unwelcome attention. But she could escape from this interference and nothing followed her out of the kitchen. The family, as Jean said, lived quite happily with their uninvited guests and the next owners were pleased to have a presence in the house.

This has been a most surprising feature of many of these stories and can be regarded as yet another refrain. The majority of the narrators eventually accepted, and even welcomed, the inexplicable forces that entered their lives.

Inevitably there have been a few contributors whose experiences were disturbing. Some of them have turned to exorcism or clearance ceremonies for help, with varying degrees of success.

Here is Hilary's story.

HILARY

We've been in this house about nine years. When we moved in, the people who had been here before us told us that three sisters had lived here in the fifties. Florence, the one who owned the house, had been widowed. She was not quite 'right' and the other two, believing that she had gone round the bend, shut her up in a single room at the top of the house. She was classed as quite mad.

Florence lived and may have died in that room. Her sisters survived her and I believe she left the house to them. The room was very claustrophobic, small and low ceilinged. When we moved in, we had the ceiling removed which gave it a gabled effect and opened it up quite a lot. It has a nice view, but it's still a low height and I can't imagine being shut up in there for possibly years on end.

My daughter chose that room to be hers because of the view and the privacy. We'd had a bit of a tough time before moving here and she was rather down. She used her room to study as well as for sleeping so she spent a fair amount of time up there. After we'd moved in she began experiencing a really bad sore throat which refused to clear up. We went to the doctor several times and, although it would sometimes ease for a little while, it always came back as severely as ever. She had never had anything like it before and it was quite upsetting.

I spoke about the situation to my friend, Jenny, who is a healer and she said, "Well, there may be something going on that is causing the problem." She offered to come to the house and find out if something negative could be causing the problem.

When she arrived, she walked through the entire house, room by room and we ended up at the top of the house, in my daughter's bedroom.

"Yes," Jenny said, "there's a really, *really* negative presence up here and I think it's causing the disturbance in her system; she is breathing this in all the time and therefore her throat is most affected."

She performed a clearance ceremony with a Bible and a cross and she asked this negative presence to move out. Within a couple of weeks, the problem with my daughter's throat completely cleared up.

It wasn't until later that I connected the story of Florence and my daughter's sore throat and I just felt that there must be something in it. There was that poor woman, possibly not mad; maybe with a condition that they didn't know how to treat in those days, shut up in that dark little room for lord knows how long, possibly grieving over the loss of her husband and not able to accept her new life with her sisters. We'll never know, will we?

Another situation where exorcism and other rituals were brought into use was in the household of Julie and her son Mark.

JULIE

I should have suspected something when the former owners of my place sold to me so quickly and moved in such haste. But I was so happy to find a flat that met all my needs that it never occurred to me anything could be wrong.

At first, everything seemed normal. My son, Mark, was living with me and my daughter stayed with us temporarily until her new house was ready. About three months after she left, things began to happen.

There was a bakery behind our building and people were always working in there. My bedroom window looked out onto it, so there was a constant soft light coming into the room.

I woke up one night to find that the dog, whose bed was at the far side of the room, was sitting by the side of my bed, whimpering. There was a very bright light and I lay quietly for a moment until I got used to it, then I sensed that someone was in the room and I turned over. There was a figure in the far corner – a young woman, quite petite, dressed in a dark cape with a large hood and a deep ruffle around the neck. She stood unmoving, looking down a little so I couldn't really see her face.

Although my heart was pounding, I didn't feel scared. I just lay there and watched her for what seemed like hours but it was probably just a few seconds. Then she moved – gliding up the room and disappearing into the wall behind my bed.

I couldn't believe it. If anybody had ever asked if I believed in ghosts, the answer would have been, "No." I tried to tell myself I'd been dreaming, but I knew that wasn't the case because the dog had woken me up. Then I thought it was probably just a one-off thing that would never happen again, so I didn't say a word to anybody.

Things began to go missing: I'd put something down and it would disappear. Mark would go to get something and it wouldn't be there. We *knew* the item should be there – but it wasn't.

And then I had another night visitor. Again I woke up to find the dog whimpering at the side of my bed. Again I turned over so the room was in my view and there, at the foot of my bed, stood a young girl. She was about eight years-old, with short, curly hair and she was wearing a smocked dress, almost like a nightdress, with little puffed sleeves.

She wasn't looking at me, but was staring at the wall just above my bed. I had a picture of my grandfather there, but I could never figure out any connection between that and the girl. I turned to follow her gaze and, when I turned back, she was gone. Just as with the first visit I didn't feel any fear and I went back to sleep.

The next time was different. I woke up and didn't even have to open my eyes – didn't have to rely on the dog – I knew someone was stood there and when I did open my eyes I saw him straight away. Him. This time it was a man. He wore a dark hat with a long black coat or cloak, I don't know which. He was old and he just stood there at the foot of my bed and I was scared. I closed my eyes tight and tried to fight the frightened feeling that had swept over me. "I don't like this," I said to myself, "I don't like this. Go away, go away, *go away*! "

When I finally opened my eyes again, he had disappeared. I still didn't say anything to Mark or anyone else because I thought it would be a one-off thing like it was with the other two: I was hoping desperately it would be like them and that he'd come to see whatever he wanted to see and that would be it. But it wasn't.

I'd gone to bed in the normal way and again I was awakened by the feeling of a presence in the room. The dog was whining and I knew that this person was close to me – this man was close by. I couldn't see him but I knew it was him because I felt scared. He came near – he came behind me and put his arms around my middle, I could *fee*l them and I was terrified. I thought, "I've got to shout to Mark," but I was absolutely frozen and couldn't get a sound out of my mouth.

The awful thing was that I could hear Mark in the living room. He was singing along to something on the TV and I needed him to come and help because I thought something drastic was going to happen to me. Somehow I managed to take a deep breath and I thought "I've got to do this and I've got to do it *now* " and I blurted out his name. It came out just as a strangled sound – "A-a-a-rk", but he heard me.

The living room door opened and I heard my son come down the hallway. He didn't know anything about what was going on but he opened my bedroom door and before I could open my mouth to say anything, he said, "You had a presence in the room, didn't you?" And I said, "Yes. Why?" And he replied, "I felt it go past me."

After that night, this presence turned on my son. He used to get choking feelings, like he was being held down by his throat. It was terrible. There were other unpleasant things that happened to both of us and we took to sleeping with all the lights on in our bedrooms.

I decided to get help and I rang a few churches in the area, but nobody would agree to perform an exorcism. They said, "We don't do that sort of thing." But I finally reached the vicar of a church in Trowbridge who agreed to visit us. He interviewed each of us separately to make sure that our stories weren't something we'd agreed upon and, after hearing what we had to say, he performed an exorcism. We were so relieved; we thought it was going to be fine, everything would go back to normal and we would be okay. We were, for about two weeks and then it all started again.

I was in despair: I wasn't sleeping and I couldn't stop thinking of what was going to happen come bedtime. I thought of staying up all night but I knew I had to go to bed because I had to work in the morning. At the time I was working in Bath, which made for a long day, so I had to get to sleep as early as I could.

After almost two years of nightly disturbances I contacted the vicar again and he agreed to come back out to us. This time he brought someone with him, a woman whom he introduced only as a friend. While he sat with us in the lounge, she walked around the house, pinpointing the troubled areas. After she was finished, she told him she thought the activity was mainly in the bedrooms, although she also detected something in a corner of the lounge.

The vicar performed an exorcism rite again, concentrating mainly on the areas she had indicated as well as going outside, which he hadn't done the first time he exorcised the place. I thought, "This is going to be it, now, because he brought someone in to identify the worst places and he's being really thorough with the ceremony."

It did seem to work because everything was quiet for about a year and then Mark said things had started happening again. I was back down in the depths and I couldn't sleep for worrying about Mark who was being harassed every night. I was also trying to cope with the sudden death of my ex-husband ; he had had a troubled life and he drowned under suspicious circumstances but nothing was ever proved.

Shortly after his death, I met with a medium who was very helpful. After going through the house, she told me that there was a doorway in my bedroom that was being blocked and that the bed should be moved to the other side of the room. She gave me a nightly ritual to perform and told me that I had to go to bed feeling strong and positive and state out loud that I wouldn't be messed around. Just doing that gave me a lot of courage.

The ritual also involved sitting on the bed and drawing an imaginary circle around the bed. She said it was a line of love and that I had to tell the spirit world that they couldn't get through this line. The first night nothing happened, but on the second night I was awakened with my whole body shaking from side to side, as if somebody was trying to wake me up, even though nobody was touching me. I didn't want to open my eyes because I was scared of what I might see, but I gathered my courage and said , "Stop it!" and the rocking stopped. It was as if something was trying to get through the circle to get to me, but they couldn't enter. I haven't had a similar disturbance since.

If you had asked me ten years ago if I believed in ghosts, I'd have said. "No." But I believe in them now. You see this programme on TV – 'Most Haunted' – where they go into houses and they see those globes. I think, "You want to come to my house and see the full thing?" It makes me laugh.

Mark is still having visitations but it's been some time since anything has happened to me and I'm sure it's because of the protective ritual I do. The medium says I have to wean myself off it, so I only do it a few times a week now, but I can't bring myself to switch the lights off. I'm afraid that if I do, everything will start over again and I couldn't bear it.

MARK

I've had a lot of strange things happen, so many that I wonder if there's something about me that makes spirits try to communicate with me.

My first experience happened when I woke up to see someone stood next to my bed. He was wearing a white monk's robe, but I couldn't see a face – it was just blanked out. I was very scared so I looked away and just lay there; when I got the nerve to look back, he was gone.

I never saw him again, but a night soon after that a woman appeared, floating above my head. She had long, blond hair and wore a white robe which swirled around her. I saw her many times, but she always kept her face turned away and I wondered if maybe she was disfigured.

One night I was standing at the top of the hallway and a young lad, dressed in an old-fashioned sailor suit, came running down the hall towards me. He disappeared halfway between this life and the afterlife.

The worst things happened many times. I'd have a feeling that someone was sitting on my chest, or pushing down on it, but I couldn't see anyone. Then there would be nights that I was paralysed – couldn't move or speak and the quilt would be pulled off the bed, or floating above it. There'd be little balls of white light shooting around the room and I could hear voices but I couldn't hear what they were saying. Sometimes the voices would come from the front room and then it sounded as if a party was going on but I was always too scared to go and look.

I had one other experience in the front room: I'd fallen asleep on the sofa and when I woke up I was paralysed, but I could open my eyes a little. There was a woman stood by the window, glowing white and I could see all the way down to her feet. It might have been the same woman I saw so often in the bedroom.

My mother had a lot of things happen to her, too, but after

the medium showed her how to protect herself, her experiences stopped. She showed me the ritual too and I tried it once but I felt like an idiot drawing a line around the bed so I just keep the light on. I feel fairly safe with the lights on and nothing has happened for quite a few months, so maybe we'll be all right now. I sure hope so.

SUE W.

I am the medium who worked with Julie and Mark during the time they were having multiple hauntings. It's some time ago now, but I remember doing some drawings for them which showed a diesel shed and some kind of passageway to Julie's house. Evidently there was a mission building there and railway workers used to visit it.

I suggested that Julie move her furniture around, which seemed to help and I also gave them a protection ritual which worked well for Julie. Mark didn't use it and I believe he is still having disturbances.

When people are particularly troubled by inexplicable occurrences they may turn to their church for explanation and help. Dom Petitpierre, an Anglican monk. who was called in for such cases and was successful in helping many troubled spirits, makes the following observations:

> In general my advice with this kind of haunt is to start from the supposition that the source is neither dangerous nor malignant but just lonely and that our spirit of friendship should be deliberately directed towards them. Yet I have found that this behaviour

> does not always necessarily work; that the departed spirits, despite their sojourn on the other side, still have hearts which have not substantially changed from what they were on earth. There are some earth-bounds, in short, who are just plain cussed – who resent the presence of successors in their beloved house.... Such people are not consciously lonely, they are not trying to get into communication with the new residents; they are, in fact, merely cross...the proper way with a departed human spirit, whether it is seeking sympathy or merely being cussed, is to ask a blessing on the house and upon the human spirit involved.

Another refrain which is present in many stories is that of disturbed places, where the house, or the area around it, had recently been altered in some way or another. It is almost as if earlier inhabitants have been activated when their ground was interfered with. This gives rise to all kinds of speculation Looking back through this collection, instances of the effects of house alterations – or a change of occupancy – are already present. But here are two more stories which graphically illustrate such suppositions.

MARTIN

When we first bought the place in Hilperton it was just an old Sunday School which had kind of turned derelict. We had to do a lot of building work which involved knocking down most of the walls downstairs and digging up all the floor.

One day we were working away – had machinery and all sorts in here – and out of the side of my eye, I saw a figure stood at the back of the house, by the back door. The walls hadn't been put in then, so you could see right through to the back.

It was a tall chap I saw, with a black beard, black coat and a big, black hat with a wide brim on it which, thinking about it, would look just as you would expect a minister to look like. I could see him quite clearly, looking sort of sideways, but when I turned and looked full on to where he was standing – there was nothing there at all.

It happened on a second occasion as well and it was in the same place by the back door. I was still working on the house and once more I saw the same figure out of the side of my eye; again, when I looked straight on, there was nothing there at all. Now, I'm not a particularly religious person, and I don't believe in ghosts or anything like that, but I did see this man.

It wasn't a scary thing at all – he just stood there looking at me, didn't seem menacing or anything like that. He was a real person, not like a shadow and that's what made me turn my head quickly to look straight at him, only to find nothing there again. Just like the first time, I saw him quite clearly, even though I was looking sideways. He was very tall and his coat went below his knees; his beard was short, black and full and the hat had a brim of at least eighteen inches across – it was a solid, wide rim. It was definitely the same person that I saw both times, but he only came twice.

My wife and I have talked about it and we think that whatever we've done to the house, he must be happy with it and didn't need to come again.

SUE S.

When all the alterations to our house in Broughton Gifford were done, we settled down to enjoy our new home. My parents used to come and stay with us for the holiday period. They'd arrive on Christmas Eve and leave the day after New

Year's. One morning, in the period between Christmas and New Year, I said to my mum, "Well, being there's all of us here, I'm going to go upstairs and clean the bathroom – it could use a good doing out." "You go on up," she said, "and I'll stay here in the kitchen and do all the vegetables."

So I ran upstairs and I was knelt down in the bathroom with the floor cloth in my hand, cleaning the lino. I could feel somebody looking at me, and I thought it was Mum. "Okay, Mum," I said, "I'll be out in a minute and then you can come in." She didn't answer me, so I thought, "Gosh, she must be dying to go; I can finish clearing up after, if she's got to go that bad." And I said, "S'all right, I'm coming out."

I stood up, threw the cloth in the basin, turned around and there was this figure stood in the doorway. I can only describe it as nun-shaped. It wasn't solid, more like a shadow – you couldn't see any features. I was *so* frightened. Then it moved – *backwards* all the way along the landing and as it went, it became more and more transparent. At the end of the landing was another bedroom, and just before it reached the bedroom door, it was gone.

I was terrified and I left the bathroom and ran down the stairs hell for leather, only to be greeted by my mother at the bottom of the stairs.

"Oh, Mum," I said, "I've had an *awful* experience!"

"Don't you talk to me about awful experiences," she said, "I've had a *terrible* experience!"

"What was it, Mum? Tell me – tell me what it was."

"You tell me first," she said, "but yours isn't *half* as bad as mine!"

"Don't kid yourself," I replied. I described everything that had happened, how the figure was there and how it backed away and all.

"Well," she said, "I can't understand that at all, our Sue, because I've had *exactly* the same thing happen to me."

And I said, "What happened?

She took me back to the kitchen: "I was doing the vegetables and I could see somebody looking at me through the door" – that door was always open – "and I turned around to say something and it was this same figure as you said and it backed all the way along the wall."

It worked out that our kitchen door is exactly dead in line with the bathroom door and where she saw it go, was along the wall to the cupboard, which was right underneath the bedroom door where I saw the figure vanish and it happened at *exactly* the same time as my sighting.

"I can't understand it, Mum," I said. "How come it should happen at the identical time? Surely a spirit can't break itself in two."

"Well, I know what I *saw*," our mum said.

"Well, *I* know what *I* saw." I said.

She was as adamant as I was and although we talked it over many times, we never were able to solve the mystery.

We lived in that house for over ten years and I always had the feeling that somebody was there on the landing and it shuddered me. The only way I could get rid of that sensation was to go into the bathroom and open the windows wide for a few minutes. When I was upstairs cleaning, I'd keep the bedroom doors shut and then I'd tear along that landing with the Hoover and you wouldn't see me for dust. Going down the stairs I was fine, but I always had one eye on the landing. I never saw the figure again – only that once.

When Richard was a little boy, he said to me, "Mummy, why do you sit on my bed in the night?" Well, I didn't but I didn't want to frighten him, so I said, "Why, don't you like me to sit on your bed then Rich?" and he'd say, "No, it scares me." And I said, "Well, I'm sorry, darling, but some nights" – because it didn't happen every night – "Mummy's got to check that you're all right." It did pacify him a little bit, but he still said, "You frighten me when you do it, Mummy."

In 1982, the last Christmas we had in the house, Mum and I

were on a two-seater settee with Richard, who was still a little boy, sitting between us. Mum and I were leaning back and Rich was perched more forward. Suddenly, I felt something push past behind me. I turned to look but I didn't see anything and then I looked at Mum who was also looking behind her.

Richard got up and left the room to get a drink or a toy – I don't remember which – and when he'd gone, Mum looked at me. "You felt it, didn't you?" she said. I said, "Yeah, did *you*?" and she said, "Yes, I did."

I felt cold, really cold and I said to my mother, "Did you feel a cold?"

"Of *course* I felt cold," she said, "wouldn't anyone feel cold experiencing that?"

Two years ago, Richard had come up from Wales. He walked in with a book in his hand and he didn't just put it on the table, he dropped it heavily. "Here you are, Mum," he said, "here's your answer."

I didn't know a bit what he was talking about. "Pardon?" I said.

"Doppelganger."

"Wha-a-t?"

"What you and me grandmother saw. It's a doppelganger – 'a ghostly double of a human form.' "

"Is it really?" I said, "Is it in there, Rich?"

He opened up the book and got the page and showed it to me.

All these years I wondered and wondered how that could happen – how one thing could be in two places at the same time, going in the same direction and everything, and now I knew.

In spite of those happenings I loved that house. I was as happy in it as the day was long and I'd live there again in a minute.

After so many stories of strange happenings and inexplicable presences, it seems time to see if there is any scientific support for such accounts. Once again Piers Bizony offers a possible explanation:

> There is currently a very vigorous debate among the most eminent scientists, the theory being that we may be living not in one universe, but an infinity of universes, superimposed on top of one another.
>
> Imagine taking a transparency photograph of a room, then hold the transparency up to the light to view it. Now, move a vase, take another photograph and lay that transparency over the first one. Next, take the flowers out of the vase and put in different ones because, in an alternative universe, you chose to use roses instead of lilies. Superimpose that transparency on top of the two you took earlier. You could go on and on, shifting chairs and tables, adding or removing a cushion or tablecloth, until you have taken many different pictures. Now – imagine those transparencies are so gossamer thin that you can see through all of them. By now you have an infinity of transparencies of today's possible outcome of this room, all laid on top of each other. This room is a shimmering cloud of alternatives which are all being played out somewhere in some universe or other. Essentially, you have the universe as it really is, but you are only conscious of one particular version.
>
> But what if you accidentally catch a glimpse of one of the transparencies that you're not 'supposed' to see? What if you get a peek at one of the alternative outcomes for this room? What if you see somebody walking through this room, right here and now, but in one of those other universes? For just a moment you are, somehow, in touch with one of the possible quantum world alternatives for this room. That may be one extremely tentative but possible explanation for ghosts.

PERIPATETIC GHOSTS

Di – Chris Bonington – Penny – Michael – David Marks
Chris – John – Robert – Kevin – Joan – Emily

So far, narrators have described events in specific places, events which frequently happened more than once. But not all occurrences are so solidly located in one spot. There seem to be peripatetic ghosts as well.

Here is one which was ready to move on with a kindly person rather than staying in the building it was already inhabiting.

DI

I moved to Trowbridge from Bradford on Avon about eleven years ago and a few years after I'd settled here a friend came to visit. She was very psychic and she got quite excited and said, "Do you realise that you've got a weaver living in your house? She stays in your living room, by the fireplace."

"No," I said, "I didn't realise it." I have sometimes felt things in places, but I'd not felt anything here.

"Oh, yes," she said, "she's wearing a big bonnet, a hessian apron and boots and she's sitting teasing cloth with a teazle."

She told me that I should find out the history of the house, if it had a connection with weavers, but I live in Newtown; the houses here were built around 1900 and hand weaving in Trowbridge would have stopped by then.

I didn't really think anything more of it and then, a while later, I was visiting this same friend and we were sitting and having a coffee and she suddenly said, "hang on – I've got your weaver here." She had a way of doing that because she was very aware of spirits and sometimes one would come with a message for me while we were in the middle of coffee or whatever. She described her in the same way as before – boots, hessian apron and bonnet, sitting with her teazles.

"Ask her about herself," I said and she said the woman told her: "Where we live there's only a few houses. We live quite near the canal, in the fields and we have cows out the back. We make butter and sell butter pats to the people who come along the canal. We're quite isolated, so there's a lot of intermarriage."

"Well," I said, "that doesn't really fit here at all. I'm not near the canal. But I suddenly remembered that when I was in Bradford on Avon, I'd lived in one of those weavers' cottages right down the bottom of the Trowbridge Road, in that little block near The Beehive, just along from the canal. And I said, "Hang on – that actually fits with where I *used* to live and those houses would have been isolated in her time, because the rest of the houses along Trowbridge Road going to Bradford are all Victorian.

She asked the woman about this and then she said, "Oh, yes. She came with you."

I'd never heard of a spirit moving with anyone and I said, "Why?"

"Well," my friend said, "she thinks you're a nice lady and you reminded her of the squire's wife." When they had problems, she said, they used to go to the squire's wife to solve them.

Apparently, even though I'm not aware of her, she's still here and she's no trouble; she just sits quietly by the living room fireplace, teasing her cloth.

Although the weaver's spirit isn't evident to me, I am very aware of other worlds and have been ever since I was a child. I grew up always knowing that if I was in a difficult place or an unpleasant situation, something was with me and I would know specifically where it was, usually somewhere up near the ceiling. I always assumed everybody had something like that but I know now that it's not the case. I've often been aware of my grandma being around me, in fact, my psychic friend once described her as a small woman, with curly grey hair, wearing a sort of blue dress. That's how she was and how I've always seen her in my mind's eye. Sometimes when I go to concerts I've been aware of Grandma sitting beside me and that's how she's dressed.

I've had several experiences of really being protected. Once, at one of the low points of my life, I was in dire straits and didn't know what to do. I was at a friend's house and feeling quite desperate and I went down the garden. Suddenly I was aware of a very tall angel standing in front of me. It folded its wings around me completely and held me and I felt enormous peace, love and warmth. When I went back into the house I said, "Okay, it's fine." Everyone thought I was barmy but I knew it was tangible, that this tall angel *had* held its wings around me and that I would be all right.

Di's description of a reassuring presence which supported her when she was under stress is not an uncommon experience. One description of such a comforting presence comes from Sir Christian Bonington, the mountaineer, during his 1985 ascent of Everest. He called it his 'supportive hallucination' and this passage is taken from his book, *Chris Bonington's Everest*, by kind permission of the author:

> I was last, but Dawa Nuru waved me past. I gathered he had run out of oxygen. I struggled up the Step,

> panting, breathless, apprehensive and then I felt what was almost the physical presence of Doug Scott. I could see his long straggly hair, the wire-rimmed glasses and could sense his reassurance and encouragement. It was as if he was pushing me on. Les, my father-in-law, was there as well. He has a quiet wisdom and great compassion. He had thrown the I Ching just before I left home and had predicted my success. This was something that had given me renewed confidence whenever I doubted my ability to make it.
>
> Doug and Les got me to the top of the Hillary Step. The others had now vanished round the corner and I seemed to have the mountain to myself. The angle eased and all I had to do was put one foot in front of the other for that last stretch to the highest point on earth. And suddenly I was there, everything on all sides dropping away below me.

This is not the only instance of a protective presence at a time of great hazard. When asked if any other mountaineers had had a similar experience, Sir Chris replied:

> In 1975 on the South West Face of Everest, Nick Estcourt was climbing the fixed ropes between Camp 4 and 5, through the night by the light of a bright moon, and noticed someone was following him a few hundred feet below, but when he reached the next camp, the other person never arrived, but he thought little of it, assuming he had turned back, but on getting back to Camp 4 he was told that no one had left the camp. The story is told in *Everest the Hard Way*. published by Hodder and Stoughton.

...Returning to West Wiltshire, Tilly, a child ghost, is of great comfort to Penny and accompanied her when she moved home. Here are Penny's experiences, together with those of her partner, Michael.

PENNY

I didn't know that Tilly came with me when I moved; I thought she had stayed behind.

She's just a little girl, about six years old and I first became aware of her soon after I'd had my daughter. My husband and I were still together then and Tilly didn't like him. She used to do things that upset him, like picking up one of my daughter's dolls and carrying it up and downstairs. All he could see was the doll and he was very disturbed. Tilly appears as a solid person to me. She's very pretty with long darkish hair and green eyes, wearing a long grey dress with a white pinny and little brown boots.

I stayed in Westbury when I left my husband. I moved to Eden Vale and from there to Leigh Park and Tilly came with me each time. She calls me 'Mummy' and she's usually with me, although once in a while she'll go with my boyfriend, Michael. Most of the time I see her, but when she doesn't want to be seen she makes herself scarce.

She's a mischievous kid and will often visit my neighbours, knocking on their doors, running down the halls, shouting, moving things. She can be quite a nuisance at home, too. One time she trashed the downstairs loo – unravelled toilet roll all over the room and spilled a bottle of bubble bath everywhere. She likes to turn taps on and she turned the grill on once – good job I went down to get a drink at two o'clock in the morning. She likes playing with the washing machine, as well.

Tilly is very observant – takes everything in. She's not used to this time; she doesn't like cars or other large pieces of machinery like forklifts, which we had outside the house for a while when there was building going on.

She's been with me for two years now. I have two lovely children, but I believe that Tilly was my child in a former life and if she left, I'd be absolutely gutted. It'd be like losing her all over again.

MICHAEL

I've been aware of Tilly's presence for the last six months, in fact I brought the subject up with Penny. I was sat down on the sofa and the temperature in the room, which is always quite warm, suddenly dropped enough for me to notice. I felt that something or someone was here and mentioned it to Penny and she told me about Tilly.

I've never seen Tilly, but I get the impression she's here and I've often physically felt her touch. One time I hadn't been sleeping well and Penny was out so I was upstairs trying to catch up on some sleep while the house was quiet. Just as I was on the verge of dropping off to sleep I felt Tilly climb up on the bed, curl up beside me and put her arm around me. That's happened a few times and a couple of times I've felt a little hand pat me on the head. Penny told me just a few days ago that Tilly was wiggling my ear while I slept, trying to get me to wake up and play, but I was oblivious.

She's usually a well-behaved child, but when she gets upset she drops a few things: you'll be in the other room and suddenly you'll hear 'BANG!' and it'll be Tilly acting up.

I don't know for sure if Penny's children see her, although the little one talks to herself quite a bit and sometimes I wonder if it's really herself she's chatting to. Penny's son is older, he's five and very observant and I'd be surprised if he hasn't seen Tilly.

Extra-sensory perception, or ESP, is a well known term. A recent study at Freiburg University in Germany, was undertaken to see if it can be proved that people do have 'a sixth sense.' One controversial theory on how such a sense can operate comes from David Marks, professor of psychology at City University, speaking on morphogenetic fields.

> They're a kind of subtle energy field that as yet we can't measure but which can, in various ways, interact between living organisms. This theory is not one that would appeal to any conventional scientists...the ideas we've seen so far are speculative.

Again, nothing can be specifically proven but that does not mean ESP does not exist. It could be argued that technological research is not yet far enough advanced to explain the phenomenon.

Animals have awarenesses beyond human capability. Insects and birds see ultra violet, so if they observe a flower they will see patterns which we cannot: they're receiving different information. Horses exhibit uneasy behaviour days before an earthquake strikes. A recent example of this comes from the Tsunami, Boxing Day 2004. There was very little loss of animal life as, sensing oncoming danger, most creatures retreated to the safety of higher ground.

Cats and dogs hear sounds which are inaudible to the human ear and apparently see things beyond the scope of human eyes. As some of the contributors have said, animals can react dramatically to what appears to be an empty space. This might not seem significant, but it becomes a curious feature when the animal always reacts in the same way at the same spot.

Human beings have not lost all their animal instincts. For many people the 'fight or flight' syndrome operates the moment that danger, physical or psychological, threatens. Adrenaline pumps through the system and the person either turns to attack or retreats as fast as possible. Some of our primitive senses may have faded, but they still exist in unrecognised or vestigial forms.

Most of us can get an uneasy sensation in one place or another. Often it can be attributed to darkness or threatening shadows; there is nothing specific to account for such responses, but such reactions persist. Here Chris puts these vague feelings into words.

CHRIS

I don't believe in ghosts; I'm more worried by the living than the dead but there have been some incidents in my life that are outside scientific explanation.

When I was fourteen years of age, I went to live with my sister Brenda and her family at Churches in Bradford on Avon. At that time, the area beyond Churches was open fields. My family always enjoyed the cornucopia of the countryside such as blackberries, mushrooms, wild asparagus, nuts and rabbits. When I lived at Churches these fields were a wonderful source of mushrooms and my sister and I often got up very early to gather them for breakfast, even though we seldom ventured into the fields alone as we both had an uneasy feeling of being watched.

Those fields have now been revealed as the site of a Roman villa, with beautiful mosaic floors. This discovery brought back many memories for Brenda and me. Perhaps because we now know of the settlement, we still feel ill at ease in those fields and I wonder if what we sense is an aura of the lives and deaths of those who lived there so long ago.

Another place of unease for me is the Westwood Road, just past the Elms Cross junction. This was the site of the Granby Hotel, which was destroyed by fire when I was a young boy. I seldom passed this area when I was a child, but my future wife lived in Westwood and, as my only form of transport was a bicycle, I often had to cycle past the entrance to the former hotel.

The hotel had been said to be haunted and whether it was hearing family conversations of this and of the fire, or if it was the eerie effect of overhanging trees, rather than riding by that area, I would deviate for about a mile towards Trowbridge and then go back on the main road. I didn't like that road then and still would not choose to walk or even drive past it on my own in the dark or, indeed, at any time.

One local road has longstanding ghostly connections. 'Sally in the Woods' is the name given to a stretch of the A363 between the Monkton Farleigh branch lane and Bathford. 'Sally' is part of the folklore of the area and has been mentioned in various books of ghostly tales. However, hearsay accounts have no place in this collection and so it has been necessary to look further into this well known story.

It is interesting that she has such a clear identity as 'Sally'. How is it that everybody knows this name? Of course, the word *sally* has a variety of meanings and it might be that the word was originally used to describe this wooded area for quite a different reason. John provides historical details

JOHN

The name 'Sally in the Woods' is a memorial to an historical event. A 'sally' was a short, sharp engagement of a defensive or information-seeking nature and the skirmish that took place in this notorious area dates back to the morning of 4 July 1643. It caused the deaths of more than fifty men from both armies on this wooded hillside.

On that summer day, the Royalist army, leaving Bradford on Avon for its proposed rendezvous at Batheaston Bridge, was ambushed at dawn by a small force of Parliamentarians under Colonel Burghill. At least 40 Cornishmen of the Royalist advance guard were killed in this sally across the river from Claverton.

This action probably had an important bearing on the ultimate outcome of the Battle of Bath, as, from this point on, the Royalist plans started to go awry. A large part of the army failed to find the rendezvous at Batheaston, and straggled to the north-west of Bath, a fact which lost the Royalist commander the choice of ground for the attack on the city. Possibly their local guides had either been killed in the ambush or had taken advantage of the confusion to take to their heels.

The action ended with the withdrawal of Colonel Burghill and his small force in order to rejoin General William Waller and the main Parliamentary army drawn up on Claverton Down.

There is little to be seen now to bring the details of this skirmish to life. However, Claverton church contains the effigy of Sir William Bassett who was the father of the Royalist Lord of the Manor in 1643 and the tombstone of Humphrey Chambers, the Puritan rector and parliamentarian in the same year. When the tomb of Ralph Allen, the quarrymaster of Combe Down, which provided so much stone for the building of Bath in the eighteenth century was opened, four soldiers who were killed in this skirmish were uncovered. Waller's trench line is still visible in Ham Meadow.

John has provided historical references, but the question of a ghostly Sally still remains. Have there been any genuine sightings?

Here is one description of an encounter with the mysterious Sally, a story which received further corroboration.

ROBERT

About twelve years ago I was driving from Monkton Farleigh, heading for home in Trowbridge. It was about half-past eleven at night and it was foul weather – absolutely tipping down with rain. The only thing I'd had to drink was tea, so I was perfectly sober as I drove my van along. It's a very nice road; you can put your foot down when it's clear, but I was being careful on account of the downpour.

I was just approaching The Fox and Hounds when I saw a woman on the left hand side of the road. She was wearing an old fashioned hooded raincoat in a dark maroon colour and the hood was up so I couldn't see her face too well.

I must have come to within five yards of her when she stepped out right in front of me. Well – I slammed the brakes on and screeched to a halt. I didn't feel a bump and I didn't hear any noise. I was rather shaken as I clambered out of the van and looked underneath it. Nobody was there. I went all around the van and searched in the ditch, but there was nothing to be seen. I thought I'd killed someone, but there was no body to be found.

I knew the area really well because I worked for the man who owned that land. "What can I do?" I thought, "I'll go across to the pub and get someone to help." And then the story of Sally In The Woods came into mind. "Well, just a minute," I said to myself, and I had another really good search around, double-checking everywhere I'd already looked. Nothing!

What should I do? Should I go and report this to the police? No. They'd either give me a breathalyser and all sorts of other tests or they'd cart me off to Devizes. So, in the end, I just went home and when I told my wife she said, "It was probably Sally In The Woods."

I never told anyone else about my experience and then, about five years later, I was coming back from Bath with Gerardo, an Italian friend of mine. Just as we came by the Fox and Hounds,

Gerardo said, "My boss, the other year, he coming down here and woman – she step straight out in road."

Gerardo's boss had had exactly the same experience as I'd had and he also thought he'd knocked the woman down. Then I told Gerardo about what had happened to me and he thought it was very strange.

Even thought this happened a long time ago, I remember it as if it was just yesterday. It was so vivid, just as if I'd really knocked someone down and killed them. I've not spoken with Gerardo's boss about it, but I certainly would like to talk to him or to anybody else who may have had the same thing happen to them with Sally In The Woods.

Although Sally in the Woods is the most famous peripatetic ghost in the West Wiltshire area, she is not alone in her wanderings. The following three stories report glimpses of other ghostly pedestrians in various parts of the district.

KEVIN

I've lived in Bradford on Avon from the time I was six years-old and, even at an early age, I didn't mix well with the Bradford kids. It was still that way when I became a teenager, but I had grown very enthusiastic about cycling and my free time was spent on my racing bike, a wonderful lightweight model that I treasured.

I'd think nothing of biking to Bristol and back, which was a sixty mile round trip, or to Warminster; another favourite ride was to the Westbury White Horse. Although I cycled a great deal on my own, I also belonged to a small cycling group and we used to do a lot of time trials which involved riding for a fixed distance in a specific time.

But on this particular occasion I was cycling on my own, heading to Bath. It was early evening and still full daylight. As I rode out of town, I went towards the old Bradford on Avon Hospital, which is on the crossroads that lead to Bath, Corsham or Trowbridge, depending on your direction.

I had just biked up the steep hill out of town and come to the crossroads when I saw a figure in the middle of the road, about two hundred feet away. "Ummm – unusual," I thought, but when its appearance registered, it seemed stranger yet. It was dressed in dark clothing, with a wide brimmed hat and a long cloak and, although I saw the figure from behind, I had the impression that it was a mature male, probably in his forties.

There was no other traffic, so I cycled straight across the road but, by the time I reached the point where the figure stood, he had vanished.

I carried on towards Bath and as I rode along I remembered that there are stories of people who walk that road and I realised that I had just seen one of them. It wasn't disturbing and was strictly a one-off experience, unlike my times with my Tithe Barn companion in my younger years.

JOAN

It was some time ago, either in the late fifties or early sixties; my husband and I were driving home from the cinema which would have made it about ten o'clock at night. We'd turned off the main Devizes-Chippenham Road, the A310, and were heading towards Melksham.

We were just passing Nonesuch, a very old house, on the left-hand side, and in the headlights I could see a figure crossing the road. I said to my husband, "Did you see something or was it just the lights?" and he said, "No, I saw this figure."

I didn't say anything about the appearance of what I'd seen, but my husband described it exactly as I'd seen it: a thin man wearing knickerbockers and a sort of Norfolk jacket, with one of those deerstalker hats with the flaps up. It just drifted across the road and into the field. We both had seen exactly the same thing; it wasn't just a figment of the headlights but it wasn't frightening.

A few days later, we were talking to someone about this and they said, "Yes, that's a common occurrence up there. There is a ghost that comes regularly from Nonesuch and is supposed to cross the fields to a cottage, where a nineteenth century poet and his wife lived."

Now, I don't know if the poet was still alive at that time, but I believe that this figure – this man – had had an affair with the poet's wife. That's all I know, except that people who take their dogs for walks in the fields opposite Nonesuch say that sometimes the dogs stop, their hackles rise and they growl as if they've seen something.

As I said, our experience wasn't frightening. My husband and I had never believed in ghosts and never saw one before or since. I never feel "Oooo, I don't want to go along that road again"; in fact , I've driven it hundreds of time since and seen nothing out of the ordinary. The memory is still very clear, but I suppose it would be as it was a most unusual occurrence.

EMILY

I've always been a bit sensitive to things that aren't of this world, so when this incident happened, I took it pretty much in my stride.

My husband Andy and I were driving from Warminster to Trowbridge, where we lived at the time. It was a cold night in January, about fourteen years ago and it was before the bypass was erected at Upton Scudamore. We passed the old farmhouse which was a familiar landmark to us. It was very dark; there were no street lights there at all, and suddenly – there she was, caught in our headlights.

She was an oldish lady, grey-haired: I'd say she was about sixty-five, neither thin nor fat, but nicely built, maybe five foot six in height. She was wearing a pleated tartan skirt and a twin set in a browny creamy colour with browny sort of squares in her skirt; no coat, and this was January, mind. She had a shopping basket on her arm and as we passed her she didn't look at us at all – just kept gazing ahead.

I said to Andy, "My God – what's an old lady doing out at this time of night, walking up the road..." and then it suddenly hit me that she really wasn't of this time.

Andy was so concerned about her that he said, "I'm going to turn around and go back there." I was looking for her in the rearview mirror and she just disappeared. I said to him, "Andy, she's not of this world – you know – she's not."

"Oh," he said and he kept on driving, heading to Trowbridge.

Now, my husband is a very caring man and, had he disbelieved me, he would have turned the car around and gone back for the old lady. But he knew that what I said was true. She looked solid, she looked real, but she was trudging up the road, dressed as if she was in the nineteen-forties with the flat kind of market baskets they used then; went past our car without even looking at it and disappeared in an area of flat fields where there was nowhere to hide.

If I'd been a woman of that age, out in such a lonely area with no lights anywhere, I'd be looking at any car that passed and trying to flag it down, but she didn't even look our way. It was like she was in her own time and walking to market.

I have the feeling that she belonged to the farmhouse and I've often thought about stopping there some time and asking the present owners if they know anything about her, but I've not done that yet.

As I said, it happened a long time ago and Andy and I haven't discussed it but I've certainly never forgotten about it and I'm sure he hasn't, either.

Sightings which have been simultaneously experienced by more than one person are particularly significant. The vivid and explicit nature of their memories adds yet another intriguing dimension which is worth serious consideration.

What does the brain take in while travelling along a road? Certainly driving, cycling or even walking can seduce the mind into relaxation. Shaun Ogbourne, whose expertise in dowsing has made him sensitive to atmospheres and surroundings, has already pointed out that when the mind is relaxed it can be receptive to other-worldly sightings

PUBLIC PLACES

Judith – Luke – Lynn – Peter -- Shaun Ogbourne – Stuart
Shane – Sally – Kerry – Shaun Ogbourne – Eleanor Macbeth
Piers Bizony – Richard – Ken – Janet – Susanne – Mary H.
Christine – Rob

Commercial buildings are likely to have many people working within them and therefore can provide more opportunities for gathering several stories from one property. For example, two such places have already been covered, one in Trowbridge and one in Bradford on Avon. The final chapter focuses even more closely on public places.

The Canal Tavern, originally an eighteenth century building, is close to a lock on the Kennet & Avon Canal. Its appearance gives no indication of the strange happenings which sometimes take place within its walls. The following accounts come from two different time periods and are baffling to all concerned.

JUDITH

I was the landlady of the Canal Tavern in Bradford on Avon from 1976 to 1988 and a number of strange experiences took place while we were there. The first one happened on a summer night. It was about eleven o'clock, and my husband and I were sitting outside after closing time, having a drink and unwinding before bedtime. The lights were on inside the house and we were suddenly surprised by the sight of shadows walking across the curtains as if people were in our living room. We rushed in and found nobody there.

Another time we were in the bar, again having a nightcap after closing time and we both heard church music. We thought it must be coming from outside, but when we opened the doors, there was nothing to be heard. We knew we were both hearing the same tune because we hummed it to each other. We found out later that there used to be a chapel on the site, many years ago.

When we were having work done in the attic, we had a huge disturbance one night. We were in bed and just nodding off to sleep when there was a great crash, so powerful that the whole room shook. My husband went up and looked around, nothing whatsoever was out of place. The noise had been so loud and the vibration so strong, that we thought a rafter had fallen down but next day, when the builders came back, they could find nothing wrong in the attic or anywhere else.

When my son was eighteen months-old and just beginning to talk he asked me who the old lady was who read him stories at night time. But that situation only lasted for a short time and I was never sure if he had been watching a story like that on television, if he was dreaming, or if there really *was* an old lady reading him bedtime stories.

Many things happened during our years at the Canal Tavern – I can't remember all the incidents – but a good example is when a potted plant that we had at the top of the stairs fell, as if it had been thrown, right to the bottom. The cat used to go ballistic, rushing out of the room for no reason and we had friends whose dogs would never stay in the kitchen. Actually, when we were in the small kitchen, which is now a utility room, we often thought that somebody was there. You'd sense shadows and if you turned around, you sometimes saw a faint outline, but there was never actually anyone there.

Our friends who had the dogs used to look after things for us whenever we went away and they would never sit in the living room when we weren't there. They didn't see anything, but they always felt cold and uneasy in there. We had other friends, too, who felt the same way but we never felt uncomfortable in the twelve years we lived and worked there.

My husband died while we were at the Canal Tavern, which is why I left there. I don't think the owner who followed us had similar experiences to ours, but I know that the present owners are having occurrences and it would be interesting to talk with them.

It is most interesting to see how many features or refrains already encountered are here again in Judith's story. There are the mysterious identical sounds heard by two people at the same time, like William and Tom; the huge disturbance at night, so similar to the one experienced by Enid and her husband; the little boy who has visits from a lady to his bedside; crashing items, missing and reappearing objects; the reaction of animals and some periods of unease. Besides being interesting in its own right, this story provides a useful reiteration of experiences already recounted.

Later events at the same property also suggest that the place has some curious other life which sometimes makes itself apparent.

LUKE

A number of things have happened to me since I began working as a barman at the Canal Tavern and I can't explain them at all. The first incident took place late one night while we were clearing away.

Pete and Lynn, the owners, and Matt, the other barman, were working on the far side of the bar and I was putting glasses away out of the glasses cleaner. I was about halfway through when I felt something go down my back. I was wearing a loose shirt and this was a firm stroke that pressed my shirt right against my back.

I was quite startled and I said, "What the hell was that?" I turned around, thinking Matt had come up behind me, trying to be funny, but he was still on the other side of the bar. Lynn could see I was puzzled; she asked me what was the matter and I told her that something had touched me.

It was totally out of the blue and although it surprised me, I didn't think too much of it at the time and we all forgot about it until the next occurrence. Ben, my brother, was working with me and, like before, I was behind the bar, standing near the coffee machine. I was wearing a T-shirt, so my arms were bare and again I felt a hand but, instead of going down my back, it stroked my arm. It was an even more intense touch than the first time, but I didn't have a big reaction to it. I turned to Ben and said, quite calmly, "The ghost touched me again."

Ben knew about the first time, but he didn't believe me; nothing had ever happened to him or to anybody else on the staff, although Lynn and Peter have had several experiences.

The next time I was touched, so to speak, wasn't really a touch at all. This time I was away from the bar area. On the other side of the pub with Lynn and a customer and while we were chatting, someone blew on my right wrist. It wasn't a breeze, it was a sharp, concentrated breath.

There were two other events that happened, both when I was behind the bar, both when the same regular customer was present. I was standing in front of the fridge where we keep the drinks and there was a loud tapping noise, like someone knocking on the glass front of the fridge. I turned around, saying, "What was that?" My customer heard it, too, but he assumed it was the motor of the fridge or something. But it wasn't – it was a definite knock on the fridge door.

The other occurrence happened in early September. My regular customer and I were talking when a woman walked through the front door. At the bottom of the steps, which you have to come down to get into the pub, there's a blind spot, so she disappeared. I got ready to serve her when she came around to the bar, except that she never came to the bar. I was watching for her and there was nowhere she could have gone without me seeing her [this was confirmed by Judith, the former landlady].

She was quite young, I'd say in her mid-twenties. I couldn't see her face because she was looking down at the floor, but she had curly hair, blondish-brown, and she was wearing a plain T-shirt and trousers – nothing you could distinguish.

My customer didn't see her because he was sitting where his back would have been to her. I didn't hear anything. I saw her come down the steps but I didn't *hear* her. I know she was there and I know she disappeared.

I can't explain these things that have happened. I don't know why they happen to me and not to anyone else on the staff and I'm not sure any of them believe me. Lynn and Peter know these events have taken place because they've had occurrences of their own and I know that things have happened when former owners lived here.

In November, I've got to stay over at the pub for a couple of nights because Lynn and Peter are going to be away and I must admit I'll be a bit wary during that time.

It's now June and, although nothing unusual happened while I was in charge of the pub last November, a number of events have occurred since and the latest was just a couple of months ago. I'd finished work a bit early one night and decided to have a tuna sandwich before heading off. I was sitting at the end of the bar with the sandwich, cut in half, with one piece on top of the other, right on the bar. As I was reaching out for it, the top half jumped off the other, flipped in the air and landed on the bar about a foot away from the other half. I was a bit shocked but after a few minutes I ate it anyway.

The Canal Tavern (top left) and main bar: the centre of the paranormal activities (See Luke's story, page 124)

Above: Westbury Swimming Pool and, left: The plaque, paying tribute to George, the friendly ghost (See Sally's story, page 137)

The Cross Guns, right, and dining room above with the enigmatic apparition (See Ken's story, page 143)

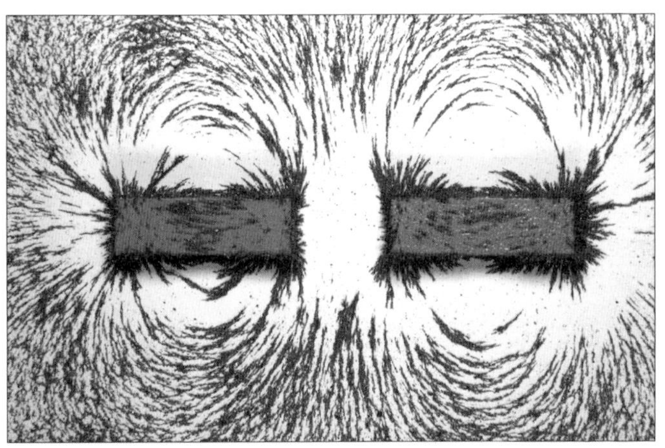

In 1850 Michael Faraday, a noted scientist, demonstrated the way in which iron filings reveal a magnetic field. This illustration is a modern recreation of Faraday's experiment (See commentary, page 152)

LYNN

The Canal Tavern has long had a reputation for being haunted, but although the past two landlords had no unusual experiences, strange events began right away with us.

Shortly after our arrival, I was awakened during the night by a noise that sounded as if someone was knocking on the wall. It was *very* loud; one – two – three knocks and then two more in quick succession.

I woke my husband, Peter, and said, "I think there's somebody downstairs. I've just heard a noise that was so loud it woke me up." Peter didn't take much notice. He looked out of the window, just to humour me, really, but he didn't see anything, so we went back to sleep.

Then, several weeks later, I was doing some gardening very early in the morning and someone hammered on the window from the inside. The noise was so loud that it really scared me. I thought it was Peter, so I rushed inside: he was nowhere to be seen downstairs but I found him up in the flat, doing some paper work in the office.

I asked him if he'd knocked on the window, but he said he hadn't. I knew that was true because the noise had come from the downstairs window in the bar and it was a very loud knock from the inside. Nobody was there; it was far too early even for the cleaner to have arrived and that's when we remembered the knocking on the wall at night and we started to think that something funny was going on.

Then, not long ago, Peter and I and Martin, the barman, were in the front bar, talking with some of the customers. One of them went to the bar to get a drink and at the same time, something went behind me and touched me on my back. It was a very firm push at the top of my back and I thought it was the customer who had done it. I turned around to say something, but he was still at the bar and there was nobody else there.

There have been a number of incidents like that and I have no idea why there's so much touching and knocking and pushing going on here. It hasn't really harmed anyone, but whatever it is certainly wants to be noticed.

PETER

I've never believed in ghosts and things like that, but what happened to me certainly made me think again. It was back last year and we'd just finished Sunday lunch. We close for a few hours after the lunch rush is over and I always go upstairs to the flat, take a shower and relax for a while until it's time to open for the evening.

On this particular day I'd had my shower and was walking back from the bathroom on my way to the bedroom. To get to it you go past the lounge and turn right. I walked by the lounge; the door was open and Lynn was in there, talking on the phone. I was just about to turn to go into the bedroom when someone pushed me right in the middle of my back. It was such a firm push that I actually went off balance and staggered a few steps.

At first I thought it was Lynn, running after me and fooling around but I realised that no way could she have got to me from where she was in those few seconds and I hadn't heard any footsteps either. I went into the bedroom and just stood there, amazed. I thought, "Wow! What on earth was that?" It wasn't Lynn; there hadn't been anyone behind me. It was *really* strange.

It hasn't happened to me again and, as far as I know, nobody else has been pushed like that. As I said, I've never believed in ghosts, but I'd certainly like to know who or what it was that sent me flying that day.

Shaun Ogbourne, who recently examined the Canal Tavern, made several discoveries which shed light on previously unconnected incidents.

> I had been asked to dowse the Canal Tavern, but hadn't been told anything about it, other than there was some activity there.
>
> I found a subterranean stream and although I didn't depth it, probably it could be a hundred feet below the surface, flowing almost the entire length of the pub, running directly below the bar and right the way along it. The upstairs alignment of the main hallway and the living space is directly above the bar. I had the impression that there might be a ghost going through the bar area, on either side and possibly upstairs, too. All the incidents there have revolved around people walking through that hallway or turning just off it.
>
> With the effects of underground water you get a field – it's not a magnetic field, but something a bit like it. Occasionally it can be deflected by geological or manmade features, but usually it rises vertically from a subterranean stream and can ascend for hundreds of feet. A good example would be a stream running underneath a tower block: you could actually get effects all the way up to the top floor. So, to have happenings on the second floor of a building as we have here, was perfectly understandable.
>
> That was my feeling about it, so it was extremely interesting to read the reports after I'd examined the areas and to discover that the activities happened in the places I pinpointed.
>
> I was not surprised to read that the people involved were either in a state of relaxation or doing a job that was so familiar it allowed their thoughts to wander.

This frame of mind lets outside influence enter easily, so it's not strange to me that Lynn heard noises that awakened her from a sound sleep or that startled her while she was gardening; that Peter had his encounter after a soothing shower and that Luke had several incidents while tending the bar at quiet times in the pub."

The next story is a good example of a practical, level-headed person who is confronted by events which have no rational explanation and manages, in part, to come to terms with them.

STUART

I'm not what you'd call a fanciful man and I was never open to paranormal experiences. I suppose I thought they were stories made up by people wanting attention I'd spent six years in the army – thought at one point it would be my career for life – but a family crisis caused me to leave. After a couple of years I joined the Wiltshire Fire Brigade as a full time firefighter and I'm still with them, when I'm not at the bakery.

It's almost two years now since I bought the Tudor Bakery and this particular incident took place a few months back. My brother, Kerry, worked with me at that time and on the day of the happening we were in the shop early to begin work.

The shop is long and narrow and the sandwich bar is at the far end, positioned so that your back is to the rest of the shop. I'd started to work on making the sandwiches and Kerry was at the front of the shop at the window, which is twenty-eight feet away. We measured it later to be sure.

I'd stacked three loaves of bread on the refrigerator/deli counter, which is on the left-hand side, ready to make up the special order sandwiches, once I'd finished the sandwiches for the window. I was busy cutting bread and spreading fillings, when suddenly I saw what I assumed to be Kerry's arm come out at my left side. I just glanced at it and kept working, when, all at once, the hand – with a two-fingered prod – pushed the three stacked loaves, which fell to the floor.

I whipped around to give my brother a scathing rebuke full of colourful language but my breath caught in my throat, because Kerry was still at the window.

I couldn't believe it: I was completely gobsmacked and my mind was in a whirl of confusion. I *knew* what I'd seen; it wasn't a blurred peripheral vision, it was a clear, full-on view of a hand with two fingers extended – a thin, white hand, including part of the forearm and a wide sleeve with no cuff but a tail that tapered about three inches. How could I have thought even for a moment that it was Kerry? The hand was nothing like his, but I suppose the mind tries to make sense of things, even when it's something that makes no sense at all.

I was so aghast, so *confused* that I didn't know what to do or say. It was three days before I even told Kerry what I'd seen because I just couldn't believe it had happened.

As I said, this happened quite a while after I took over the bakery and I'm not sure why the hand waited until then to make itself known. It hasn't appeared again, but there's something else that occurs with some regularity.

I thought of them as strobe lights, even though they didn't pulsate, but recently I was told that they're called orbs and evidently they're quite common where psychic phenomena take place. I always see them in the same position, next to the top left hand corner of the big refrigerator. They appear in groups of three or four, usually one large one with several smaller orbs. The first time it happened I reckoned it was an electrical fault but then I thought, "Hang on – you're a firefighter, you've seen big time electrical sparks and they're nothing like this."

They started to happen about the same time as the appearance of the hand but, unlike it, they keep returning. In fact, just ten days after I first told my story, I saw another one. I'd been in the small kitchen at the back of the shop, collecting pies and pasties from the fridge to place in the window. The entrance to the kitchen has one of those veils made of plastic strips and to exit the kitchen you take a step downwards and simultaneously sweep the veil aside. As I did this, I saw the orb. It was in the same place that the others had been, but it was on its own, not part of the clusters I'd seen before. It was the biggest I'd seen yet, about six inches across and although the sightings only last for a fraction of a second, this one seemed to be visible for a little longer than the others had been.

As I think about it, my reaction was very calm – not blasé, but very accepting of what I'd seen. I remember thinking: "Oh, look, another strobe." Then I remembered and corrected myself. "No, no – they have a name, they're called 'orbs'. I've just seen another orb!"

The orbs always come in the afternoon, when the shop is open. I don't know if anyone else has seen them, and I don't know if they'll continue to appear. The thought of them returning doesn't bother me at all, but I'd be quite happy not to see the hand again.

Stuart is convinced that he has seen something that is not from this world and has tried to make sense of it. His explicit description of the hand and its sleeve is astonishing – especially when he had such an antipathy to anything involving ghosts. It also appears to be a classic example of orb-sighting, the kind of occurrence which Vernon experienced in his home.

One public building in Trowbridge, which was Peewee's Real Ale Bar at the time, has already been covered in the Poltergeist section. This building shares the same substructure as The Shires Shopping Centre, both being built on the site of the twelfth century Trowbridge Castle. As the map on page 2 shows, part of these grounds contained many burials, some of which are still in place. Nowadays The Shires is an alive and busy place when crowded with shoppers but Shane, who was often there after working hours, is aware of a different atmosphere when the precinct closes down.

SHANE

I have worked as a spiritualist for many years and have had many encounters with those from the other side. I've lived all my life in Trowbridge and, fittingly enough, many of my early experiences happened at The Shires Shopping Centre.

It's often said that The Shires is haunted; many of the security guards can back that statement up and at night some interesting things have been caught on the security cameras. I was lucky enough to have seen some of the footage which someone borrowed from the security office. It showed figures flitting about; actually skitting through the cameras. I could see white, hazy outlines of people, and it was absolutely fascinating.

My Mum used to work at Argos and I'd meet her there every night at five o'clock. It was very quiet at that time, only the workers would be there, stacking shelves and so forth, and they'd let me in to pick my mother up.

One evening, waiting for closing time, I was stood outside what was then The Dutch Bakery – it's another bakery now – and I felt somebody tapping me on the shoulder. I saw nothing at first; then, out of the corner of my eye, I saw someone shuffling past. It was a man, wearing a very dirty, grey cape with the hood pulled up over his head and as he passed I got a strong whiff of manure. I turned to face him but, as I did, the figure was completely gone and the smell went with him.

The Shires was built on the site of Trowbridge Castle – you can see a display of the castle at the museum in the shopping centre – and the main street of the castle ran down to where

Argos is. The castle gates were where the Argos pick-up point is now. Most of The Shires' spirit activity takes place in the area that leads from the museum, including the passage from Argos down to Asda. There's a feeling of solemness – of *weight* – in that part of The Shires and there have been many encounters there.

As time went on, I met the caped figure again and what I picked up was that he'd been a street cleaner. Delivery carts were always heading to the castle and when items fell off – dead animals, pigs, apples, whatever – he'd pick them up and put them in the storehouse that stood on the site of the Dutch Bakery. He'd also clean up the horse manure, which would be stored at the side of the railings which go around the bakery.

There are other spirits from that time who are active in The Shires. They usually show themselves as an outline; sometimes I see their faces very clearly, but they're almost transparent. I have spoken to them; sometimes they respond positively and sometimes they're negative. I've helped some of them to leave, but many of them are still trapped within The Shires.

There are many other haunted spots in the central area of Trowbridge: they may not be as well documented as The Shires, but they're no less real.

Another much frequented place is Westbury Swimming Pool. It has a reputation for being haunted, so much so that the ghost has long been given a name, thus becoming a familiar part of the establishment.

Sally has had numerous encounters with this being which, over the years, she has learned to take in her stride.

SALLY

The Westbury Swimming Pool, which was built in 1887, is well-known as a place filled with paranormal activity. There used to be a Roman villa under the pool itself and it had a central heating hypocaust system which was quite common to those times. In the late fifties or early sixties, they were extensively explored by a team of archaeologists.

From the late Victorian period to the early Edwardian years, there was a caretaker who worked at the pool for at least twenty years and he lived on the premises, sleeping on a canvas cot in an annex to the boiler room. He died in that room, and when he was found, there were hundreds of old newspapers stacked against the walls. He was a local man and members of his family, who still live in Westbury, are understandably reluctant to have his real name used, so he is always referred to as 'George'.

I have been a caretaker at the Westbury Swimming Pool for twenty-five years. When I first began working there they had just started to modify the building and in the annex I saw the cot, the newspapers and other bits and pieces of a person's sad life, still lying there. The manager had begun working at the pool at the same time as me and he told me that there was a funny atmosphere in the plant room. He also said that a spanner had flown off the wall and floated past his head.

I used to begin work at 3 a.m. with the rest of the staff arriving around six, which meant I was alone in the building much of the time. If it was a rainy, windy day, I used to feel that someone was standing behind me. This happened a lot, not just to me, but to other staff members, too.

The first time I saw George, I was hoovering on the balcony above the pool where there had been a party the night before. There were other staff in the building, but I was alone in the area. While I was hoovering around the railing, something made me look down. I saw a man standing by the doorway to the men's changing room. At first I thought he was maintenance staff but no maintenance appointment had been made and the front door was locked so nobody could enter, so I wondered how the heck he got in. He was completely real looking, wearing a baggy navy blue boiler suit and big hobnailed boots. His hair was silver and very untidy and he had a heavy growth of stubble. He looked up and caught my eye and I stood there and stared at him. He stood motionless and then moved and gazed down at the water.

I was frozen and I called out, "Julie, there's someone let themselves in here." He suddenly turned around and walked straight into the wall. My heart pounded crazily and I thought, "I'm seeing things." But I knew what I'd seen. A minute later, Julie stuck her head out of the ladies' changing room and said, "What do you want?"

"Blooming heck," I said, "I thought some man had let himself into the building, but he just disappeared into the wall!"

"Oh, my God!" she said.

We searched all around but found nothing. I rang the manager and he said, "Oh, that'd be George." He'd seen him many times and was aware of his presence at many other times.

Many of the other staff have since seen him and there have been other events there, too. Julie was in the ladies' changing room when all the locker doors suddenly opened and then closed loudly, one after the other, which gave her an enormous fright. This still happens and quite often we have trouble with the hoses in the ladies' room, too. They're kept on reels on the wall and often I'll put the hoses away after using them for cleaning the changing rooms and when the manager comes to check, the hoses will be unreeled all the way down the floor and the cupboard doors will be unlocked. Another frequent happening is when the life-saving poles, which are securely hooked to the wall of the pool area, spring off within seconds of each other and fall to the floor.

Just two weeks ago, the duty officer came out of his office.

He was completely unnerved and said to me, "Come and see this – the blinds have been going up and down, up and down." When I went into the office, the blinds had stopped moving, but were still vibrating. "It's only George," I told him. "He won't hurt you."

During the war, the pool was covered over and used for tea dances and roller skating and we have often heard big band music from that era coming from the pool area. Many times, too, we've heard the sounds of children laughing and playing at the pool when the building is closed.

I've seen George about five times at the pool and it's always on rainy, windy days, but there are many occasion when I just feel a presence. Also, again in rainy weather, I'll often be in the pool area and will hear three loud bangs on the wall, as if someone is on the outside catwalk, but when I go to look, nobody is there.

At one time, the West Wiltshire District Council didn't like any mention made of George or the other happenings at the pool. They were concerned that it would frighten the children but, over time, children and adults alike have been so fascinated that they've changed their position to the point where we now have a sign outside the pool saying that, along with its Victorian heritage, we have George, 'a friendly ghost'.

It is noticeable that Sally's initial response was to freeze, which mirrors the reaction of Michelle and Julie in earlier stories. It is also interesting that George is described to everyone as a 'friendly ghost' and is considered an attraction for the building.

Although fictional ghosts are often presented as unpleasant and frightening – and people often enjoy being frightened – the situations in this book show ghosts as often quite benign. The next account also supports the suggestion that ghosts do not have to be the creepy, hostile creatures of myth and legend.

KERRY

Back in the early nineties I was a security guard. I was a mobile guard, which meant that I had various places to check on a regular basis and one of those was Heywood House in Yarnbrook. It's a huge old building and it was used as the National Trust headquarters for this area.

Monday through Saturday my routine took me there at six o'clock in the morning where I unlocked the building, including many of the interior doors. I'd open various windows and make sure that all was in order, then leave for my next assignment and come back at five or six o'clock in the evening, depending on how quickly I got my other duties done. I'd make sure that everyone was out of the building, that everything was clear and then I'd lock it all down for the night.

The day this happened, I remember, was a lovely summer's morning, bright and already hot. I was running a little bit late and arrived there at about half-past six. I opened the main door right away, as usual, and then went around the whole building, checking in various areas. The thing about this house was that the further you went into it, the darker it was, because the interior rooms didn't have windows to the outside.

I was about forty-five minutes into my check which meant I was deep in the heart of the building and it was very dark. I'd always turn the lights on as I went into each area and I'd just entered this particular part of the house when I caught a movement out of the side of my eye. It was...it's a difficult thing to describe...it was a human shape and it seemed to turn and face me as I entered the room. I couldn't tell whether it was male or female – there was no outline of hair, as it were, just an indication of head, shoulders and body – like a silhouette, except it wasn't dark. It was something like a television set without a signal, when you've got a snowy picture; it flickered like that, but it was *clear*, you could almost see through it.

It was only about ten feet away from me and I just stood there, *staring* at it, it must have been for nearly a minute. It didn't move at all, it just stood there and I felt enormous peace – a sense of great *ease*. There was a strange scent around it, a woody smell, like an old log that's been lying long on the earth.

It sounds bizarre, but when I thought I'd stared at it long enough, I just nodded to it, walked around it, went on to the next room and carried on my duties.

I didn't tell anyone what had happened: I thought, "Well, that was for me." And that's how it stayed, until now.

Kerry's sighting could be an illustration of physical matter, interpreted in a similar manner from three different points of view.

> *Shaun Ogbourne:*
> I've heard that electromagnetic force can be a frequency or it can actually be matter – that it can change from a particle to a wave and that it can go right through the universe like e-mails do. I think that these are just two ways in which energies present themselves. I believe that there are many kinds of energies and that if scientists were to take more notice, they would find ways of detecting them.

> *Eleanor Macbeth:*
> Matter at its most broken down form, isn't solid. It's information held in waves that become solid as we observe them. An atom is mostly not a particle at all, it's mainly gaps between the particles and when subatomic particles are broken down there are masses of space between them. Anything we perceive as solid is mostly empty space and the reason we perceive it as solid is because of an interaction between this

information and our nervous system which has developed over aeons.

It's a bit like tuning a radio into different frequencies. When people begin to see things, they start to pick up on different frequencies of light; in physical terms we are basically made up of electromagnetic forces holding particles together. These particles are charged and when they move they create an electromagnetic field and that's what healers feel or – if they see auras – that is what they observe. Interestingly, the magnetic parts of the electromagnetic field of a human can be measured with scientific instruments to a distance of fifteen feet from the body.

Piers Bizony:
The tiniest bits of matter, clunking against each other, interacting and then flying off in different directions; no matter how far they fly apart, if you fiddle around with one of those pieces that has had a relationship with one of those other pieces – instantaneously, the other piece, far, far across the universe, knows about it and immediately changes its shape correspondingly. It's as though once bits of the cosmos at this subatomic level have had some kind of relationship – some kind of interaction – they're always linked. It's a bit like radios that are partly tuned in to a station and you half catch something on the airways. We may be getting little glimpses from far, far away where particles that were once joined with our particles are sending information back to us.

Kerry had never told his story to anyone until he brought it forward for this publication. As he said, it remained a private experience. But there was a curious follow up when one of the authors of this book read his story out to a group at an evening gathering. Astonishingly, after the session, one of the audience came forward to say she had already heard this story. It was told to her some forty years ago by a policeman attached to Warminster Police Station who had had the same experience. He had even described the same smell surrounding the vision. Although this was only hearsay on her part, and therefore cannot be regarded as a first-hand narration as all the other stories are, it is extraordinary to have this unexpected corroboration – especially since the session was in a totally different part of West Wiltshire.

The closing stories come from an inn noted for paranormal activities. These accounts from The Cross Guns in Avoncliff are of considerable interest in that they span a period of fifteen years with several narrators being involved during that time. Landlords, chefs, bar and serving staff have had a variety of experiences while working in this venerable building and there appears to be no end to the happenings here.

KEN

I was told that The Cross Guns was haunted before I bought the place, which was five years ago last April. It houses the spirit of a Victorian lady, who has been seen in several different parts of the pub as well as in the grounds, and many members of the staff have had encounters with her as well as with other spirits who make The Cross Guns their home.

Janet, one of our cooks, first saw the Blue Lady, as she is known, ten years ago when she first worked here. Janet left The Cross Guns for some time and recently returned to work with us. She met the Blue Lady once more shortly after her return and saw her again just a few weeks ago.

Our chef, Rob, who also returned a short while ago, worked here when Janet first did and he has had many experiences with our other-worldly residents. Several other members of the staff have seen not only the Blue Lady, but also a man in a monk-like habit and an elderly gent who apparently walks through the beer salon into the bar.

But it's the Blue Lady who is seen most frequently, by staff and customers. One woman, sitting with a group at the dining table by the old inglenook fireplace, saw her briefly but clearly, almost in the blink of an eye. She was intrigued and has come back with several colleagues but her husband refused to return. Sadly, she hasn't seen the Blue Lady again.

We are situated by the Avon river and the Kennet & Avon Canal. Before the canal was dug, you could walk behind the pub and past the stables which provided the only means of transport at that time. The Blue Lady, who presumably walked down that path, now steps out of the wall of the Ladies' washroom, often giving a nasty shock to anyone in there at the time; I'm aware of six or seven customers who have had such an encounter, some of whom ran screaming back into the pub and some who were fascinated and brought friends back with them to see if they, too, would see her.

Personally, I've only had one paranormal experience here, which had nothing to do with the Blue Lady. It happened about three years ago, when I was working on a website project with a photographer. We had to wait until late at night, when the pub was empty, to get clear shots of the rooms and while the photographer was working, two strange, lingering images began to hover around head height at different spots in the pub. My first thought was that it was smoke, but nobody was smoking, nor were there any spotlights on. We took several shots of them with the digital camera and the results have been interpreted differently by almost everyone who has seen them.

Although I've not seen the Blue Lady or any of the other apparitions, except for the one pictured, I believe in the many experiences that staff and customers have had and, apparently, are still having.

JANET

I began working at The Cross Guns ten years ago and it was during that time that I first saw what we call the Blue Lady. I was in the loo and she came out of the wall and walked through me, which was a very unsettling experience. I was quite upset, but most people didn't take much notice of what had happened to me. Then a few days later a fisherman came in and said to Dave, the landlord, "Did you know that you have a ghost here?"

Dave asked him to describe what he'd seen and he said "Well, she was dressed all in blue." This was exactly what I'd said and, as the fisherman and I had never seen each other before, Dave realised that what I'd seen wasn't a figment of my imagination.

After that, things started happening in the kitchens, which made the chefs uptight; they were hearing things and sensing disturbances. They didn't really believe in what was going on, but it upset everybody so much that they called somebody in and did – not an exorcism, exactly – but a leading to the light. This quietened things down and, as I left for another job, I didn't hear anything more.

I was gone from The Cross Guns for eight years and came back just a few months ago. There's still lots of strange goings on; something seems to happen just about every week. I saw the Blue Lady again and this time she spoke to me. Evidently people were making up names for her and she didn't like that at all, in fact, she was quite annoyed in a rather comical way. She told me her name is Georgia but I didn't hear her out loud, it was more like her voice came inside my head.

The Blue Lady always lets you know that she's here. The air starts to go cold – not in the usual way where you yourself feel chilled – the cold is all *around* you, like there's a presence there. Georgia is often here and when I see her I see *all* of her, from her bonnet right to her shoes which are buttoned and laced in that old style. She has very large, brown eyes – staring wide open. Her bonnet is big and her gown has a very full skirt. I think she's around twenty-three or twenty-four and I have the impression, maybe from her, that she was jilted: I believe she was a commoner and a man of the gentry brought her here and left her and that she's wandered around here ever since.

She hasn't frightened me since that first time and I think I'd quite miss her if she wasn't here.

SUSANNE

I worked as commis chef at The Cross Guns tens years ago, doing the starters and the sweets. Part of my job, last thing at night, was to take the food from the kitchen into the cellar which we used as a cold room – a pantry, if you like. I always stored everything away carefully – the meats on one shelf, vegetables and salads in another part, cooked items in a separate area; it was always laid out very nice and I enjoyed seeing it all neatly placed and ready for the next day.

One night, as I was walking down into the cold room, I felt a strange sensation – I can't describe it any other way than that, except it was cold, much colder than the room normally was. Still, I shrugged it off and started to put food on one of the shelves but as I was bending down, out of the corner of my eye I saw something move. It looked like the back of a leg dressed in something blue and I had caught sight of it in mid stride. It disappeared into the beer cellar, which was beyond the cold room and had only one door.

A couple of nights earlier, I'd disturbed two boys who were pinching beer. I thought they'd come back to try their luck again, so I quickly gave chase. I couldn't see anyone there. I pushed the door open and looked all around, even behind the beer barrels in case they were hiding there – but no, there was nothing, nor did I hear footsteps or any other sound.

I went back to putting the food away and, when I came out of the cellar, I told one of the waitresses what I'd seen. She didn't take a lot of notice and I put it behind me, telling myself that I must have imagined it. But the following weekend, Rob, who was the chef, told me about an incident that had happened to Janet who had been working behind the bar that evening. She'd gone to the ladies' loo and seen what we now know as the Blue Lady.

When I heard that, I realised that I'd probably had the first sighting of her, even though my view was a limited one. From what I hear, she's shown herself to many people since then. It's quite a while since I worked at The Cross Guns, but I'll never forget the experience I had there.

MARY H.

Most of the things that happen to me take place in the kitchen, but one night, I reckon it was six weeks ago, Janet and I were sat by the front door. It was a warm evening, but the door was shut to stop the nits coming in, so it was very warm inside. Suddenly, I said to Janet, "I'm cold – really, *really* cold." There were goosebumps all over my arms and the cold air was all around me. It stayed that way for a good twenty minutes.

Janet wasn't cold at all, but she saw a shadow pass through. It wasn't the Blue Lady. I didn't see anything, I just sat there, frozen all over and when Janet put her arm out to me, she could feel the cold air surrounding me, just like what used to happen to Bev [a former barmaid] when she worked here.

A couple of months ago I was laying a table out just across from the window and I saw someone there, wearing a light coat and floating, like. It was just there for a few seconds and then it was gone. But, like I said, most things I've known have happened in the kitchen. One night I heard a woman talking to me, right in my ear. I was busy working at the time and it took me a moment to realise that there was nobody there, just the woman's voice, so close.

Things go missing a lot as well, like our two favourite kitchen knives. We didn't know where they'd gone and figured they must have been thrown out, although it's not like any of us to be careless with good knives. But one night, a week later, Janet turned around and saw that one of the knives had been placed right across the rubbish bin. It certainly wasn't there before because we'd been there all night and would have seen it.

Then, just last week, I was about to come out the kitchen door and I felt something hit me lightly on my back. I thought it was the chef, Rob, and I said to him, "Stop throwing things at me."

"I never," he said and he hadn't. There was nothing on the floor, nothing at all, but I certainly felt something hit the middle of my back.

It may sound silly, but so much goes on that you learn to live with it and you actually forget some of the things that happen. It's just part of your day.

CHRISTINE

I've been working at The Cross Guns for fifteen years and I was on duty with Janet the night she first saw the Blue Lady. She came running into the pub quite hysterical. I thought she'd been attacked by somebody but she said she'd seem something walk through the wall in the ladies' toilet. It took us quite a while to calm her down.

Janet described her as dressed all in blue, in her early twenties, with big, brown, staring eyes. She had to go through her to get out the door and she said it felt awful. She said the woman wore little ankle boots and when she was coming back up to the pub she could hear the little 'click clack' behind her as if the Blue Lady was following her. Nobody else on the staff has had an encounter with her except Janet, but customers have seen her, as well as some of the fishermen and boat people who are moored close by on the canal.

The only thing I've seen is the woman who stood in the kitchen doorway. It wasn't the Blue Lady but a big, solid looking woman – Rob said she looked like a housekeeper. That happened about two months ago and Rob and I both saw her at the same time. He was in the kitchen and I was taking a break, sitting at a table where I could see into the kitchen from a mirror. It was so fast – only a second or two – but I saw her, real as could be, from the back and Rob saw her from the front. We could see each other's faces, too, looking absolutely gobsmacked. It was really scary and I'm happy not to have seen anything else.

ROB

I've been the chef at The Cross Guns for a long time, worked here off and on for years. There's lots that goes on here, lots that I've seen, lots that I've heard and lots that other people have experienced, staff and customers alike.

Seeing the Blue Lady is what happens often and although I've never seen her, I was here when Janet, one of our cooks, saw her for the first time. I thought she'd been attacked by someone, but she said she'd seen something walk through the wall in the ladies' loo and that she'd had to go through it to get out of the door.

That same night the phone kept ringing, the staff kept answering, but there was nobody there. We called BT who said that the line was clear, but it was dead, except for the calls. I finally lost my temper and shouted down the phone "What's going on? Don't keep phoning us!" And then this young voice said "I'm cold. I'm wet. I want to sit by the fire." My hair stood straight up on end and I hung up. But the call came again and again – three times within about five minutes and each time it was that young girl's voice, saying the same thing.

One of the strangest things happened a couple of months ago. It was lunchtime and I was taking a tray of chicken out of the oven, so I had my back to the door. Suddenly something told me to look towards the door and there stood the figure of a woman. She looked like an old-fashioned housekeeper and although she was only there for the blink of an eye, I saw her very clearly. The really peculiar part was that Chris was sitting in the next room; she was looking into the kitchen through a mirror on the wall and she saw the woman at the same time, but from the back. Chris and I could also see each other's stunned faces in the mirror and we both said at the same moment "Did you *see* that?!"

But there've been other things I've seen that nobody else has. A couple of weeks after seeing the woman, I was coming down from the bar. It was fairly late and so quiet that Ken had been all alone at the front. He was behind the bar and as I passed there I saw an old chap sitting in the booth opposite, with a pint in his hand, chatting to Ken who seemed to be looking at him.

I said to the girls, "Don't worry – Ken's got someone to talk to, he's not on his own any more.

"Who?" they said.

"The old gentlemen that's sitting up there with him now."

"No one's there with Ken," they said.

"I'm not mad," I told them, "There's an old man, sitting talking to Ken, pint in his hand."

I saw him very clearly. He was wearing a greenish-greyish suit, sort of 1940's type. I thought Ken had been looking at him, but it turned out he was looking towards the girls here at the back and the only one who saw the old man was me. I only saw him that one time, but we had a lady working here who used to see an old man go into the cellar. Maybe it was the same one.

But, like I said, lots of things go on in The Cross Guns. Years ago, during my first time here, the place was owned by Dave. His daughter and son-in-law and their little girl, Emily, were here, too. Emily was only two years-old and we had an intercom in the kitchen because her mum, Mandy, worked down here and that way she could keep a check on her. We all used to hear Emily playing with an imaginary friend; Mandy would run upstairs to tell her to be quiet and go to sleep. Emily would bawl her eyes out but as soon as Mandy left the room, she'd be giggling and laughing again.

None of us thought too much of it; children often have imaginary playmates, right? But one day when Emily and her parents were out, Dave went upstairs and he came flying down again saying that all the toys had come alive. We all ran up to Emily's room and every toy was working on its own as if they'd all been wound up at the same time – whistles were going, bells were ringing, the lot!

After that, they called the church and the Dean of Salisbury and some expert came and did an exorcism. We went through every room in the place, the toilets, everything. But it didn't work, because things are still going on as much as ever. Big, bulky shadows go across the kitchen or stand next to the sink. I see them quite often and as long as they don't approach me from the side but come at me head on, I can deal with it and I always say good night to them.

I think one of them might be Dougie. He was the odd job man, a big man in his fifties. He went into hospital for an operation on his knee and he died. He always worked here in the back, bleaching the stone floor or at the sink, pulling up buckets of water. He was always around, even when he wasn't working and I think he came back after he died because he always liked it here. I like it, too, even with all what happens here. I never used to believe in such things but I do now and I manage to live with it all.

Such a wealth of sightings suggests this place contains some curious and persistent force which goes beyond the rational and visible. It would seem that there is some kind of 'field' within which energies, invisible most of the time, have their being. This may sound unlikely but there ***are*** invisible forces which govern our planet and the entire universe, the most obvious one being that of gravity. We cannot actually ***see*** it, but we know that it controls our bodies and the world we live in.

Another such force field is the electromagnetic one. Again, although it is not apparent to the naked eye, it can be explicitly demonstrated and captured in experiments and photographs. Perhaps The Cross Guns is at the centre of a different but analogous force field connected with the paranormal. This is only a speculation, but something is needed to explain so many accounts over time by such a variety of people.

CONCLUSION

What can be learned from these stories which people have so generously contributed?

Here, for the first time, is a collection of the events experienced by some of West Wiltshire's inhabitants and described in their own words. There are no inventions and, wherever possible, corroboration has been obtained. The quality and integrity of the narrators is also significant, with nothing being set up to 'make something happen'. People are simply going about their daily affairs when something inexplicable makes itself manifest. The reader may find some stories more plausible than others, but it is clear that contributors have carried the memory of these events as genuine happenings, never to be forgotten.

Because this book is a collection of first person experiences, it is more than just another anthology of ghost stories. Even though many accounts have some similar points of reference, each one is very personal and has its own individual features. There are a few instances of unpleasant occurrences which have caused distress but, these were very much in the minority because most people's reactions were more positive than expected. Some treated the inexplicable in a matter-of-fact way, taking the strangest situations in their stride, while others welcomed the unusual and even enjoyed a 'presence' in the house, describing feelings of acceptance, peace or even pleasure. The study of this material has thus produced one conclusion which is quite reassuring.

Ghosthunting is a constant in film and television entertainment, as well as in story form, and accounts of ghosts have always been popular. They frequently contain a fearful element, based on the assumption that people enjoy being frightened when sitting in the security of their own homes. But this emphasis on the disturbing may well be an unfair depiction of these other worldly beings.

The ones in these stories do not seem, in general, to contain any particularly aggressive qualities: they are simply *there,* and contributors have responded accordingly.

But have we learned what ghosts actually *are*? Do we know, after reading these experiences, that ghosts really exist? Earlier generations were much more convinced than we are today. The Victorians were particularly involved with the afterlife. Perhaps in that century when untimely death was so frequent, such messages from 'the other side' brought them comfort. But we live in a more cynical age and we search for proof.

Today's world, full of ever changing technology, would have been beyond the belief of anyone living a hundred years ago. What would our ancestors have made of the mobile phone? The notion that someone in Melksham could lie in her bath at midnight and talk to her daughter walking on a beach in New Zealand would have seemed either impossible or else something straight from the spirit world. All the stories recounted in this book involve some form of energy, frequently coming from inexplicable sources. Although no rational explanation can be offered as yet, it does not necessarily follow that the events did not take place.

We know that we are surrounded by energy waves because we are used to the ways in which radio and television operate. Technicians can now harness electro-magnetic energies in all kinds of other ways – websites, e-mails and laser technology, for example – which demonstrate in everyday terms how potent and malleable this invisible force can be. There is no doubt that energy creates effects that extend far beyond our present understanding and may well be responsible for mysterious experiences such as those recounted in this book.

Can we, in the twenty-first century, dismiss the inexplicable? Can we truly know what is real and what is not? The questioning of reality is nothing new. How to resolve it is a fundamental difficulty which was apparent to the great philosopher Descartes, grappling with the same question in the seventeenth century. His conclusion was: 'Whether I am awake or sleeping, two and three added together always make five and a square never has more than four sides; and it does not seem possible that truths so apparent can be suspected of any falsity or uncertainty.'

The mathematical certainties Descartes relied on continue to be the foundation for investigation of physical forces. Einstein influenced all scientific perception of the universe with his revolutionary formula $E=mc^2$ where E = Energy, m equals Mass and c equals speed of light (186,000 miles per second).

Quantum physics takes this equation even further by making clear, through mathematical proof and scientific research, that energy changes form. It reacts to what is around it and can become a particle or a wave. It can be manifest as light, heat, sound or movement. Modern scientists tell us that the universe has no empty space, it is full to bursting with cosmic energy. Richard Feynman, one of the world's most brilliant theoretical physicists and the acclaimed author of *QED The Strange Theory of Light and Matter*, gives us this breathtaking statement; 'the energy in a single cubic metre of space is enough to boil all the oceans of the world.'

With such extraordinary statements coming from world renowned scientists, it seems arrogant to dismiss anything we cannot, at present, explain or replicate to order. Although there is little scientific support for much of what has been described in these stories, it is hoped that sufficient emphasis has been placed on the dramatic leaps in technology and the peculiar ways in which quantum physics seems to be moving, to suggest that clarification will eventually emerge.

During the compilation of *Hosts of Ghosts,* many other stories came into consideration but, regrettably, time and space prevented their inclusion. Further material was excluded because the events occurred outside West Wiltshire. Interestingly, they illustrated many of the same aspects as the local stories. Dom Petitpierre also provided examples of the paranormal events he was called in to investigate which exhibited similar features throughout the country. It is evident from all the material which has been gathered together that the selection presented here reflects curious happenings which extend well beyond West Wiltshire.

FURTHER READING

SCIENTIFIC

BODANIS, David. *E=mc2: A Biography of the World's Most Famous Equation*, MacMillan, 2000

BIZONY, Piers: *Invisible Worlds: Exploring the Unseen,* Weidenfeld & Nicolson, 2004

FEYNMAN, Richard P: *QED: The Strange Theory of Light and Matter,* Penguin Books, 1990

GREGORY, Richard: *Eye and Brain*, Oxford University Press, 5th edition. 1998

GRIBBIN, John: *Quantum Physics: A Beginner's Guide to the Subatomic World*, Dorling Kindersley, 2002

McTAGGART, Lynne: *The Field*, Element – an imprint of HarperCollinsPublishers, 2001

GENERAL

BONINGTON, Sir Christian: *Chris Bonington's Everest*, Weidenfeld & Nicolson, 2002

DESCARTES, Rene: *Discourse on Method and the Meditations*, Penguin Books, 1968

GRAHAM, Alan H & DAVIES Susan M.: *Excavations in Trowbridge, Wiltshire, 1977 & 1986 – 1988,* Dorset Press for Wessex Archaeology, 1993.

PETITPIERRE, Dom Robert, O.S.B.: *Exorcising Devils*, Robert Hale Ltd, 1976 (O/P)

ACKNOWLEDGEMENTS

Several people from different backgrounds and with differing points of view have contributed their knowledge to this book.

Sophie Barnes was a nurse for many years, which complemented her skills as a healer; she now works as a counsellor. She has been aware of the supernatural since childhood and this knowledge has had a strong influence on her life.

Award-winning writer and journalist Piers Bizony has covered a wide range of popular subjects including quantum physics, cosmology and space exploration. He is a non-believer in the paranormal. Nevertheless, he has been most generous with his time, and very helpful in explaining some of the basics of these hugely important scientific developments as they may impinge on the strange accounts which follow.

Eleanor Macbeth has always had an understanding of the properties of energy. She obtained her MA in Zoology at Oxford and, after training and working as a physical therapist, she spent a year studying energy medicine. Her practice includes physical and energy-based treatment of her clients.

Shaun Ogbourne is Chairman and an active member of the Wyvern Dowsers Society. With his skills and knowledge he traces water and energy channels which lie far below the ground and gives advice on the effects these may have on land and buildings.

Dom Petitpierre OSB was an Anglican monk and a leading Church of England authority on ghosts and what he called 'place-imprints'. He travelled the country as part of his ministry of healing and deliverance. His book, *Exorcising Devils*, now unfortunately out of print, contains a large number of examples of strange visitations, many of which accord with the ones collected here. Through his religious belief and vast experience in this field, he built a Christian philosophy to account for inexplicable events.

Special thanks to: Ritka Carr who designed the cover for Hosts of Ghosts; Michelle Slade who was of great help in the collection of material from Westbury; Jackie Tollit who photographed several of the sites in the book; Mark Wright who formatted the manuscript.

ABOUT THE AUTHORS

Margaret (Maggie) Dobson

It seems some unknown force gradually propelled me into the curious subject of ghosts. As an English Tourist Board Guide, a local hotel asked me if I would create a ghost tour of Bradford on Avon near to Halloween for some important visitors. It was only June, and so I lightheartedly agreed, only realising much later when I came to create the tour that it was quite a challenge. To make sure that the evening would not be entirely fanciful, I asked various friends if they had ever had any ghostly experiences in the town. To my surprise, several of them – sensible, down-to-earth-people – said that they had. These stories became part of the evening's entertainment, the visitors enjoyed themselves, and I then put the subject out of my mind.

But some months later, a speaker was suddenly needed for a morning event and I found I was volunteered to give a talk on 'Ghosts and Spirits in Bradford on Avon.' Rational people naturally want to hear more than a ghost story – they want to know why it happened. In trying to find some simple kind of framework for the talk, I went into Quantum Physics – and quickly came out again. But by this time my disbelief in ghosts was beginning to be challenged – especially when the coffee morning produced more strange stories from the audience. Although by now intrigued by these personal accounts from trustworthy people, I felt the subject was once again closed.

The next event was an invitation from Roger Jones to consider writing a book of local ghost stories. This I declined, recognising the amount of hard work needed to produce something worth reading. But the final persuasion came from Simone Brightstein who was most keen to collect more material and was ready to share the many months of effort which always lie behind any published writing.

It has certainly been a most interesting exploration of worlds previously unknown to me. I still don't understand them, but my sense of wonder at the complexities of the universe has increased ten-fold as a result.

Simone Brightstein

Maggie Dobson was one of the first people I met when I moved to Bradford on Avon five years ago. I admired her work, both as Chairman of the Preservation Trust and as the author of *Bradford Voices* and was delighted when we became friends.

I had recently completed my first novel and was receiving the usual lack of interest that the publishing world gives to most new authors. Nevertheless, I had begun on a sequel but I quickly hit a writer's block the size of Mount Everest.

One evening, during this dry period, I had a few friends, including Maggie, to dinner. Earlier in the week she had given her talk on ghosts in Bradford on Avon which I had missed and I insisted on a total replay, so Maggie had to serve up her stories with every course. We were all fascinated but when I said that she should write a book on the subject, she blanched in horror.

But I couldn't shake the idea that there was a good book in there somewhere and, although my fictional writing was going badly, I was sure that, together with Maggie, I could do a decent job on the ghosts of the area. Accordingly, I invited myself over to her house on a Sunday morning, girded up for what I thought would be an enormous battle of wills.

When I broached the subject, saying that I would be happy to work with her, Maggie told me that she'd had a letter from Ex Libris publisher Roger Jones, asking her to write a ghost book. She had refused, but after considerable persuasion from me and further thought, she agreed to join forces.

Strangely, as soon as I began to work on the book, I received an offer of publication for my novel.

I have come out of this journey neither more believing nor disbelieving in ghosts than when we began; my mind has always been open on the subject. I have greatly enjoyed working with Maggie and I have been touched by the trust our contributors have shown us.

More books from Ex Libris Press:

WILTSHIRE & SOMERSET

AVONCLIFF by Nick McCamley; £9.95

FILLING SPACES by Stan Hey; £5.99

BRADFORD VOICES by Margaret Dobson; £9.95

HIDDEN DEPTHS by Isobel Geddes; £9.95

WHERE WILTSHIRE MEETS SOMERSET by Roger Jones; £5.95

Also available:

COLLIERS WAY: History and Walks in the Somerset Coalfield, by Peter Collier; £6.95

CURIOUS WILTSHIRE by Mary Delorme; £7.95

THE DAY RETURNS by John Chandler; £9.95

THE GEOLOGY OF SOMERSET by Peter Hardy; £9.95

THE MARLBOROUGH DOWNS by Ken Watts; £9.95

THE SOMERSET LEVELS by Robin & Romy Williams; £.9.95

THE VALE OF PEWSEY by John Chandler; £7.95

THE WEST MENDIP WAY by Derek Moyes; £5.95

All these books may be obtained through your local bookshop and are always in stock at EX LIBRIS, 1 The Shambles, Bradford on Avon, BA15 1JS. Tel 01225 863595